PH WORDS

STUDENT'S USER MANUAL

WITH ACCESS CODE

Fall 2003 Update

PEARSON
Prentice Hall

PRENTICE HALL, UPPER SADDLE RIVER, NEW JERSEY 07458

PEARSON
Prentice Hall

©2004 by PEARSON EDUCATION, INC.
Upper Saddle River, New Jersey 07458

All rights reserved

10 9 8 7 6 5 4 3 2 1

ISBN 0-13-184907-7

Printed in the United States of America

TABLE OF CONTENTS

WELCOME TO PH WORDS 4
QUICK START 5
SYSTEM REQUIREMENTS 6
REGISTRATION PROCESS/STUDENT LOGIN 7
    NEW USER BUTTON 8
    ACCES CODE 9
    USER NAME AND PASSWORD 10
    CONFIRMATION SCREEN 11
    LOGIN SCREEN 12
    COURSE CODE 13
    COURSE LISTING SCREEN 14
SYLLABUS SCREEN 15
SYLLABUS ICONS 16
DIAGNOSTICS 17
INSTRUCTOR MESSAGES 22
PRINTING THE SYLLABUS 24
COURSE CONTENT 25
WATCH VIDEO 26
RECALL SCREEN 28
MULTIPLE CHOICE APPLY SCREEN 31
APPLY EXERCISES IN GRAMMAR MODULES 35
    INSTRUCTION BUTTON 36
    TOOLBAR ICONS 37
    HINTS 39
    SOCRED PERFORMANCE DETAILS 41
WRITE EXERCISES 42
ASSIGNMENT VIEW 43
    DIAGRAMS 44
FEEDBACK VIEW 46
GRADEBOOK SCREEN 47
    GRADEBOOK REPORT 48
MESSAGES SCREEN 50
    CREATING MESSAGES 51
    READING MESSAGES 52
MANAGING MESSAGES 53
PRODUCT HELP FOR BOTH INSTRUCTORS AND STUDENTS 54
PH WORDS DEVELOPMENT TEAM 55

Welcome to PH Words!

PH Words is a Web-based course in English. It allows you to study writing and grammar and then reinforce what you have learned in a variety of exercises specially designed for use on a computer. To do all of this, you must first register for the course through your school, and you must be able to use a computer that has access to the Internet through Internet Explorer. Finding PH Words on line is as easy as typing in any Inernet address.

Once you are set up to use PH Words, your teacher may give you a diagnostic test to determine your areas of strength and weakness. Your teacher will assign exercises for you to complete on the computer, and then he or she will be able to see your work on line and provide feedback. You both will be able to keep track of your progress electronically. In addition, if you get stuck, you can send a message to your teacher explaining your problem or asking your question.

When you use PH Words, you will be using cutting-edge technology designed to help you develop your writing skills. Your teacher wll be able to supplement classroom material, and you will be able to work outside the classroom on a computer at school or at home.

For the most recent information and updates on PH Words, visit
www.phwords.com/support

Quick Start

If this is your first time using PH Words, skip this page and follow the instructions on the next few pages.

If you are already registered and set up for a course in PH Words, follow these easy steps to start working:

- Login and click the **OK** button.
- On the Syllabus, click the **Chapter** you want to work on.
- Click the **Section** you want to work on.
- Click the **Module** you want to work on.
- On the **Exercise** screen, read the instructions and answer the questions.
- Click **Done** to submit your work.

SYSTEM REQUIREMENTS

If you are not sure if your computer can provide access to PH Words, here are the Windows System Requirements:

- Pentium Class or higher CPU, 266mHz or faster

- 32 bit operating system (Windows 98, Windows NT 4.0, Windows 2000, Windows Millennium Edition or Windows XP)

- 64 MB RAM

- 800x600 or greater resolution, 256 colors or greater

- Minimum consistent Internet Connection speed of 56k

- Internet Explorer 6

- Sound and speakers

- Macromedia Flash Player version 6 (web browser plug-in)

FOR TECHNICAL SUPPORT, PLEASE CALL THE
PRENTICE HALL MEDIA SUPPORT LINE
1-800-677-6337
MONDAY THROUGH FRIDAY
8:00 AM TO 5:00 PM CST
OR E-MAIL US AT
media.support@pearsoned.com

STUDENT LOGIN

1. First, connect to the Internet, then open the **Internet Explorer** browser.

2. Type the address, www.phwords.com into the address line, and hit **Enter** on your keyboard.

3. When you see the PH Words welcome screen, click the **Start Here** button.

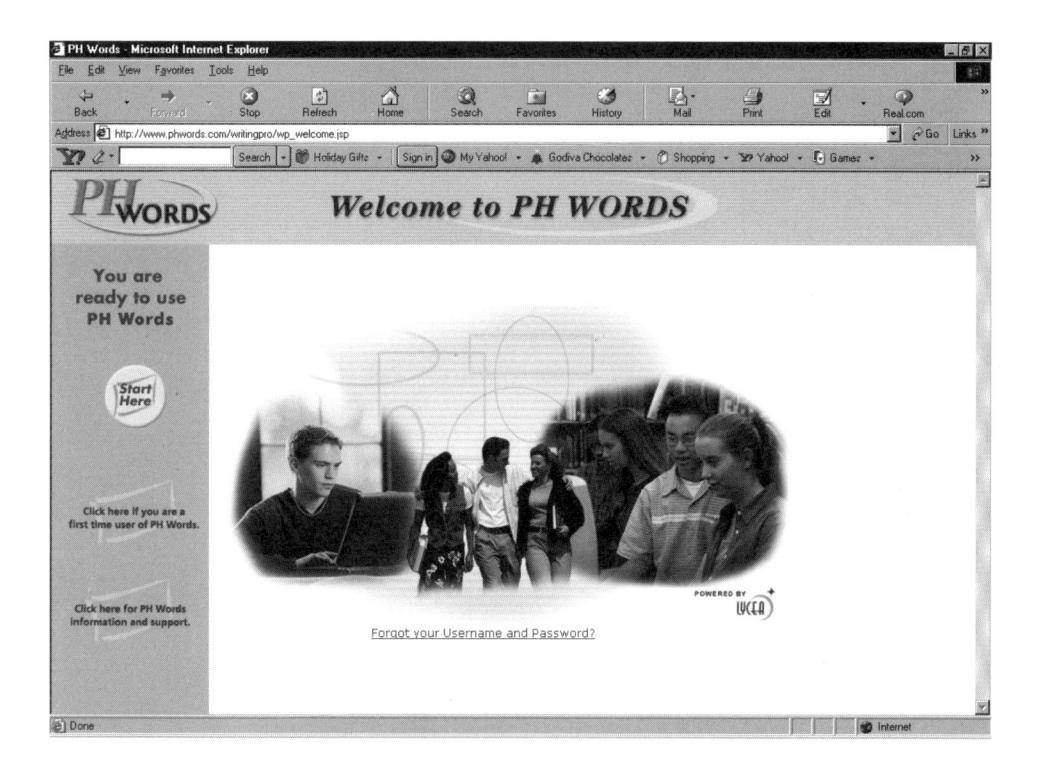

4. If this is the first time you have connected to PH Words, click the **New User** button below the password box to register. You will have to do this only one time. This leads you to the **Registration Screen**.

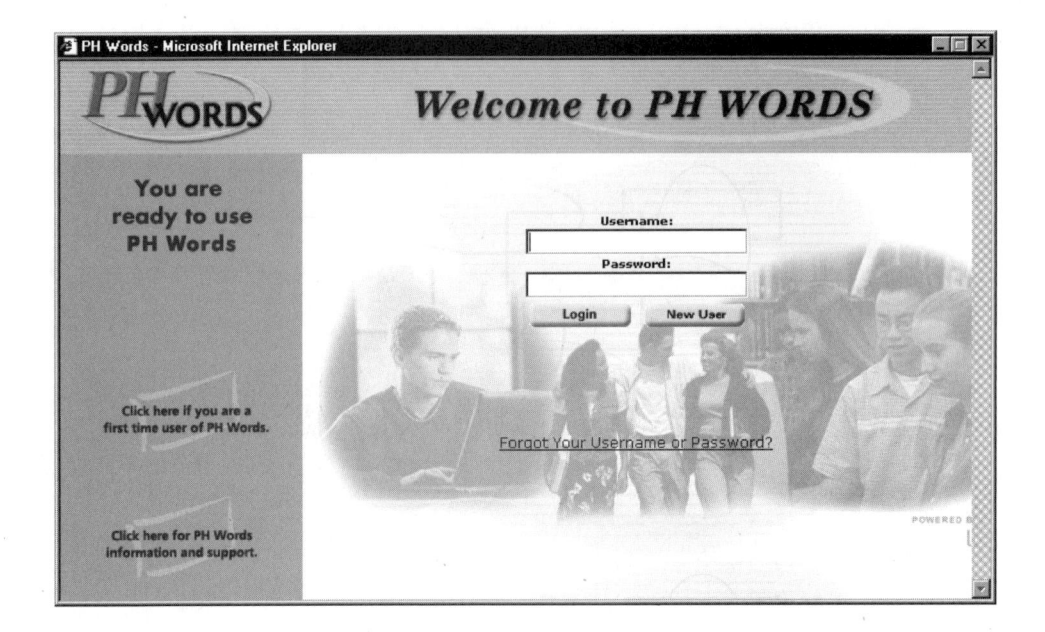

5. Enter the **Access Code**, a six-word code you will find inside the front cover of this Manual. It will look something like this: PHWDED-PUPAE-MILKS-TIGON-NABIS-CARST. The words don't meaning anything and they are not case sensitive, but they must be entered exactly or the computer will not recognize them. Choose **NO, I am a new user** and click **Next**.

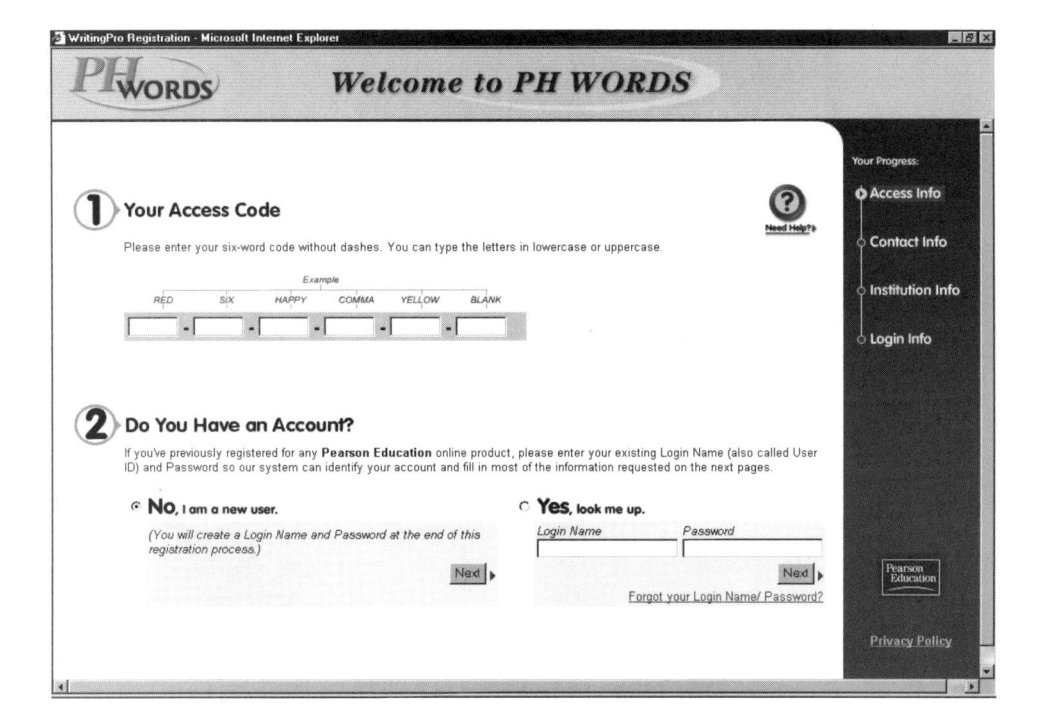

6. Follow the instructions you will see on the screen. Again, be sure to enter all the information accurately, including your e-mail address. During this process, you will create your own **Username** and **Password**. Write these down because you will need to use them every time you want to return to PH Words. Make sure to click the **I agree** box under License Agreement before clicking **Next**.

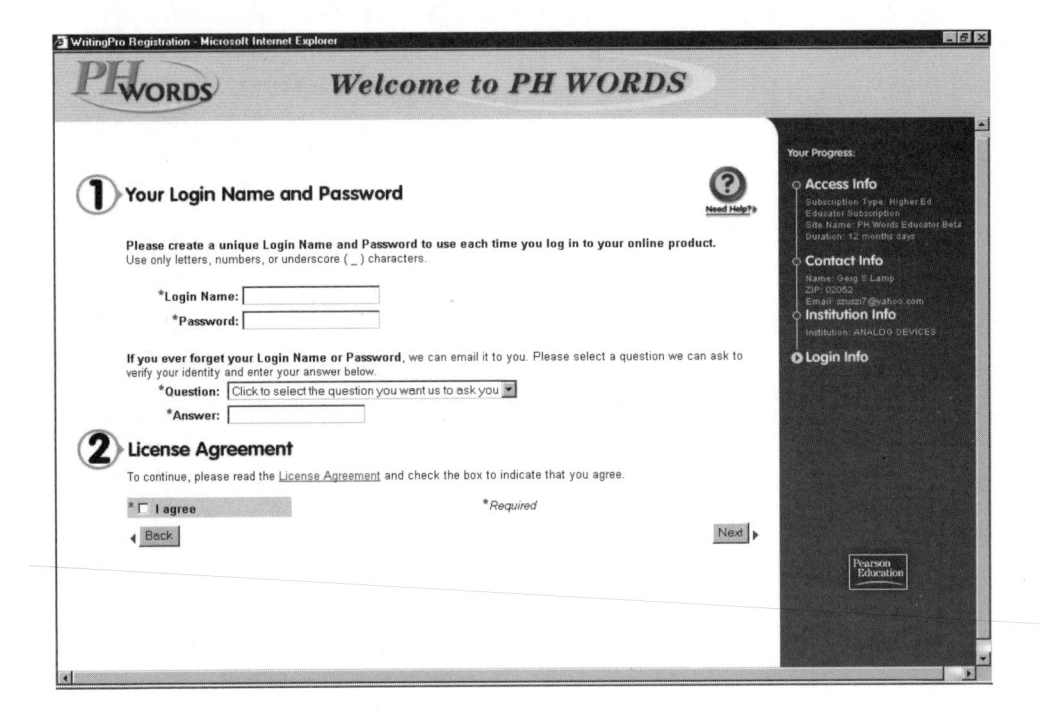

7. You will then move to a **Confirmation** screen that summarizes your course information. You will need to refer to this information subsequently, so you may want to print this page for your records. A confirmation with this information will also be sent to the e-mail address you provided.

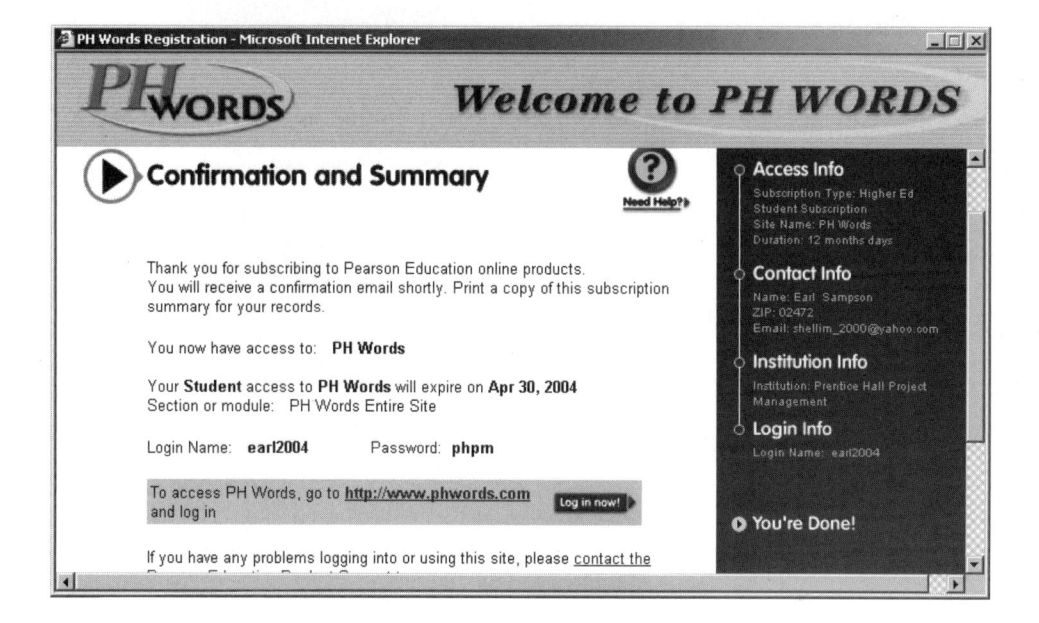

8. After you have registered, click on the **Login Now** box to return to the **Login** screen. Enter the **Username** and **Password** that you have just created.

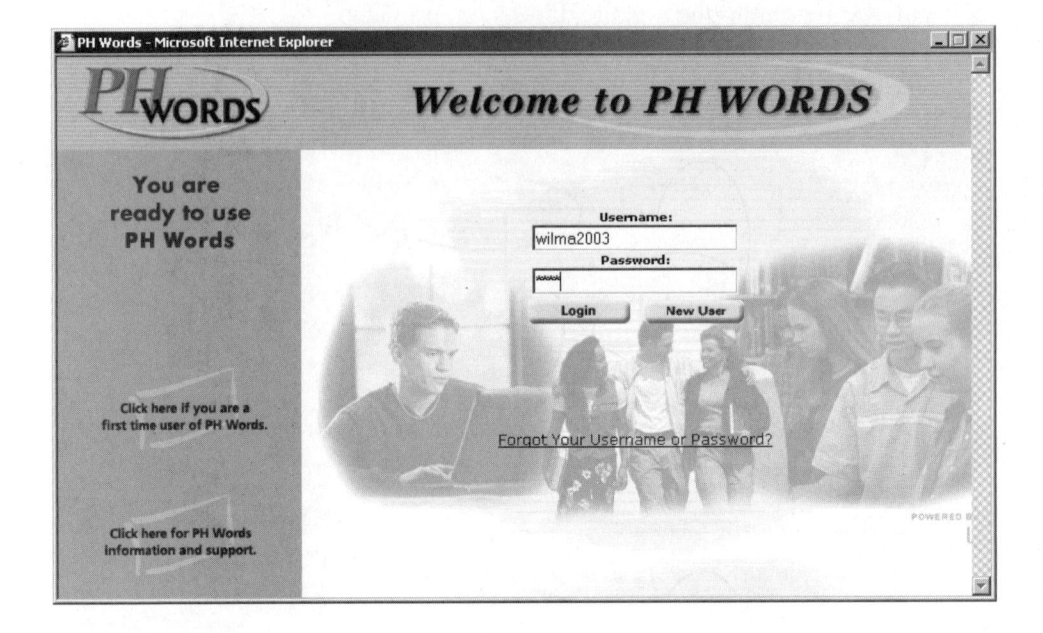

9. Now that you have registered—and each time you return to PH Words—you will have to type in your **Username** and **Password** and then click **Login** to begin your session. You will be asked for the Course Code only the first time, when you register. If you do not know this code, you will have to ask your instructor to provide it for you.

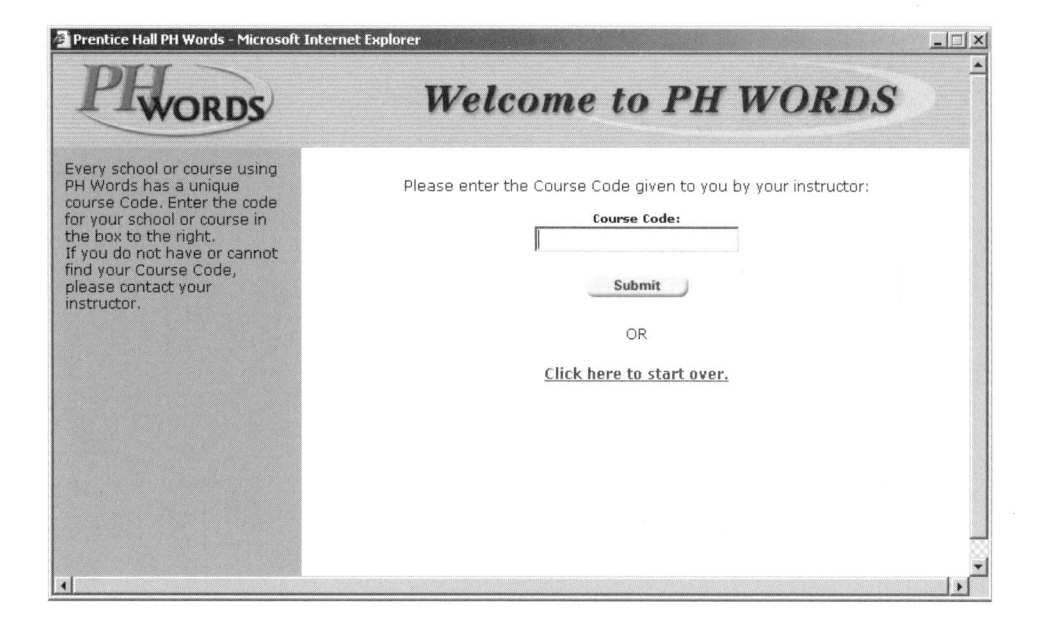

10. The next screen you will see is your own **Courses** screen, which lists all the online PH courses your have registered for. For each course, there are screens that link you to **Syllabus**, **Gradebook**, and **Messages**. The Messages link indicates how many unread messages you have. There is also a **Help** button to open a general **Help Menu**.

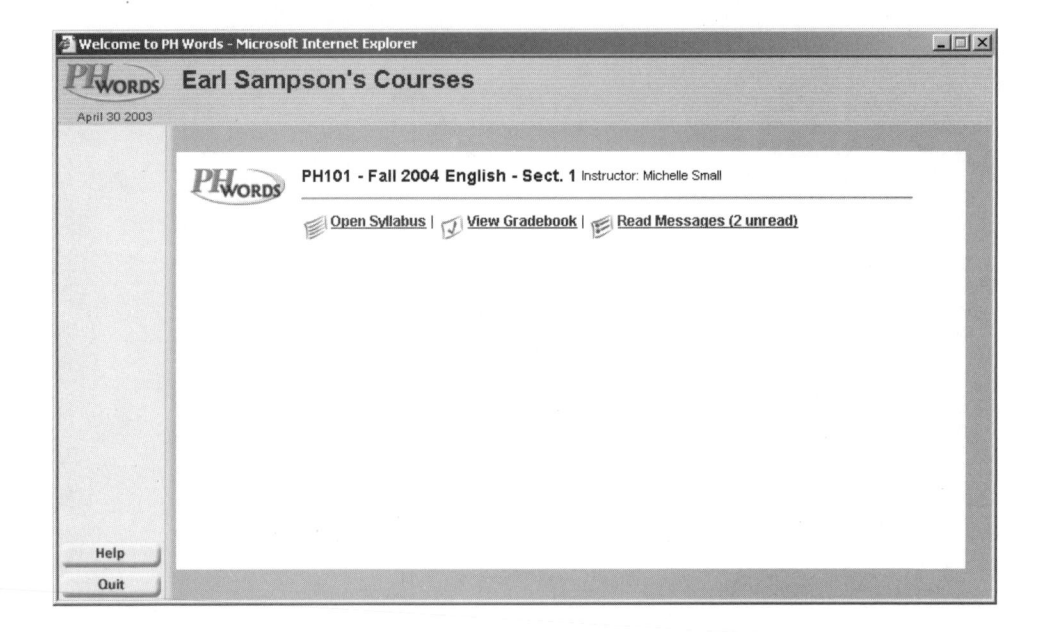

SYLLABUS SCREEN

The **Syllabus** is your home base, allowing access to all material in the course and providing an overview of the whole course as well as your progress through its content.

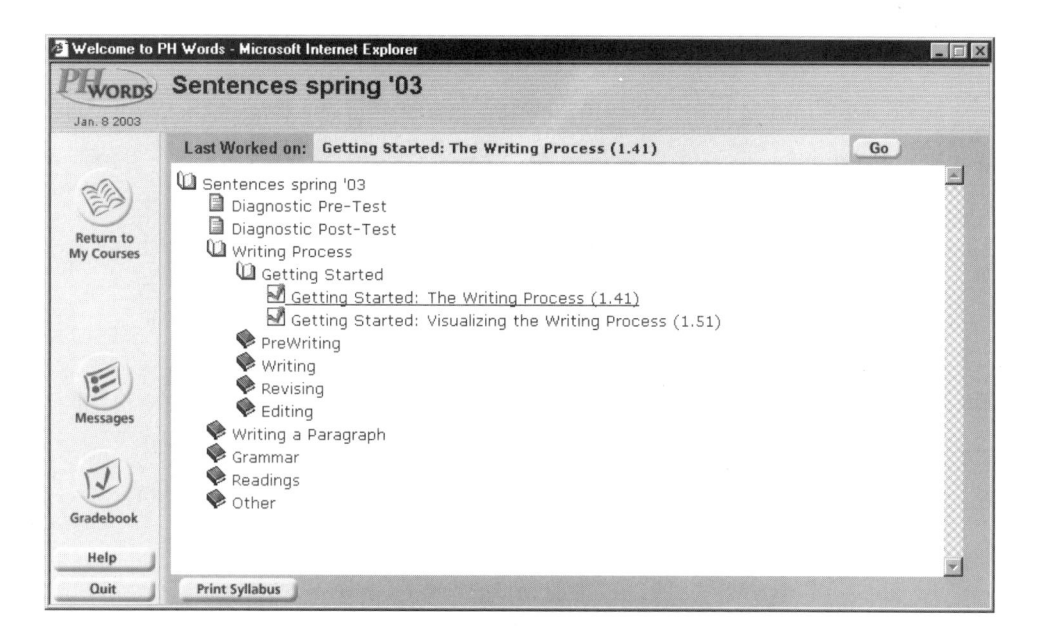

Through the **Syllabus**, you can get to the spot where you want to work and you'll usually return to the **Syllabus** after completing an item. The screen shows the last item worked on, and you can return to it instantly by clicking the **Go** button.

You can also open your **Gradebook** or **Messages** from the **Syllabus** screen by clicking either of these buttons on the left side of the screen.

Syllabus Icons

A closed book signifies that items are available under this heading in the Syllabus, but are not being displayed. Click the book to see what's hidden.

An open book signifies that all the items under this heading in the Syllabus are displayed.

A book with a checkmark signifies that you have completed all the items under this heading.

A page with writing on it represents an item that you have not yet completed.

A page with a blue checkmark says that you have completed the item.

A page with a green checkmark says that you have mastered the item, either through the diagnostic test or by completing the exercises.

A page with an "S" means you have submitted work for this module to your professor. Once he or she has graded it the "S" will turn into a checkmark to show that you have mastered the item.

A page with a "G" means that the instructor has graded the item and you may click on the link to read the comments.

A page with a blue and yellow **I** signifies that there is an instructor note attached to this item.

DIAGNOSTIC TESTING

PH Words includes optional Diagnostic Pre- and Post-Tests covering grammar and punctuation skills. Your teacher will decide if these tests are to be included in your syllabus. Your teacher will use these test results to provide you with a customized learning plan through your Syllabus. Diagnostic test scores are also logged in the **Gradebook,** but they are not counted toward your grade.

When you open your Syllabus, if your teacher has chosen to include the pre- and post-tests, you will see them as the first items in your syllabus.

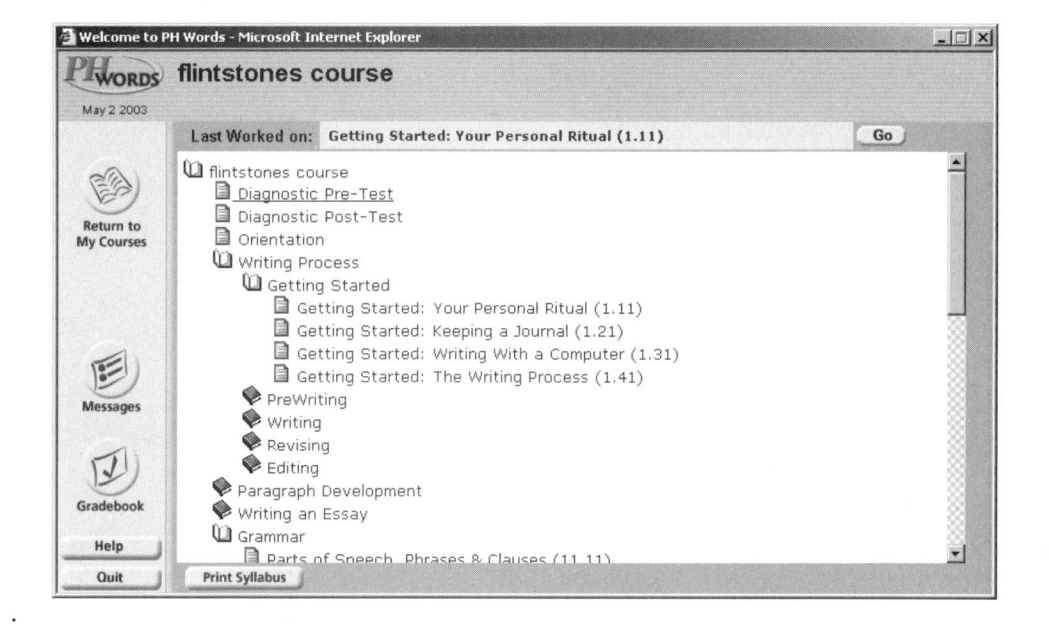

As soon as you click on the Diagnostic Pre-Test item in your syllabus, a message will appear.

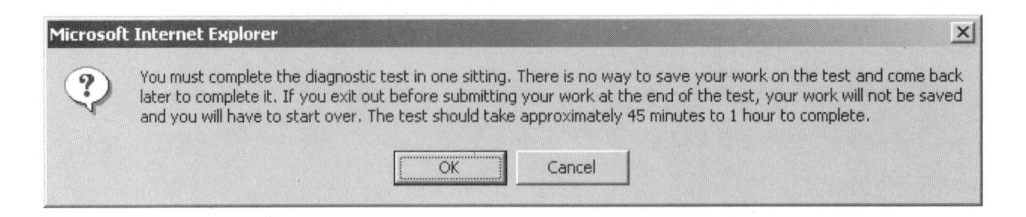

> **Microsoft Internet Explorer**
>
> You must complete the diagnostic test in one sitting. There is no way to save your work on the test and come back later to complete it. If you exit out before submitting your work at the end of the test, your work will not be saved and you will have to start over. The test should take approximately 45 minutes to 1 hour to complete.
>
> [OK]   [Cancel]

This message is **VERY IMPORTANT**!

Both the Diagnostic Pre-Test and the Post-Test **MUST BE COMPLETED IN ONE SITTING**. There is no way to save your work and come back later. If you exit from the test before completing it, you will lose all your work and nothing will be recorded in the Gradebook. If you exit by hitting the **Submit** button, your score will be calculated on whatever work you have completed, and there is no way to go back and finish the test.

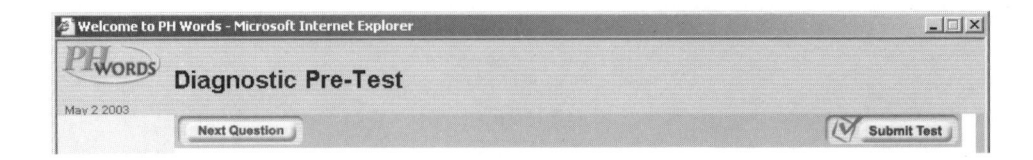

> **Welcome to PH Words - Microsoft Internet Explorer**
>
> PH WORDS **Diagnostic Pre-Test**
> May 2 2003
> [Next Question]   [Submit Test]

However, when you have completed the DiagnosticTest, ou must remember to hit the**Submit** button in the upper right hand corner for your grade to be recorded.

The diagnostic test questions are all multiple choice. You must answer each question in order, and you cannot skip any questions. In determining your answer to a question, you can change switch back and forth among the various answer choices as many times as you like—until you are sure of your answer; at this point, you click the **Next Question** button.

When you have completed all of the questions, click the **Submit Test** button to send your score to the Gradebook and automatically place your score in the **Diagnostic Pre-Test Gradebook** report.

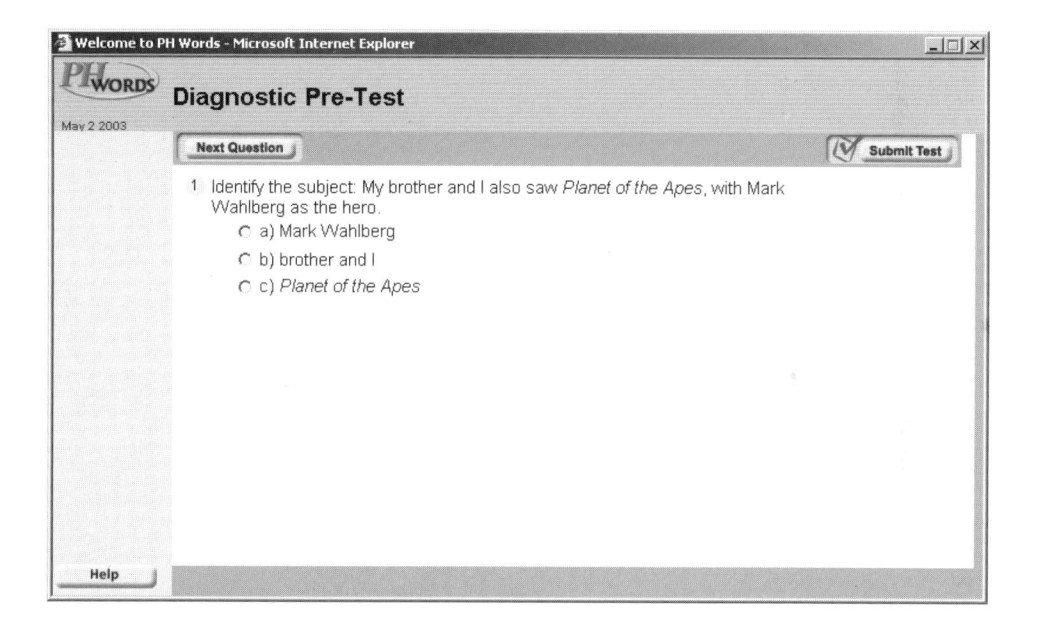

You will also see a summary page showing how many of your answers were correct and how many were incorrect. (Note: in the example here, the student got all of the visible questions correct. A red x will appear next to any question that you get incorrect). You can then go back into the pre-test to review the questions that you had difficulty with. However, you will not be able to change any of your answers at this point.

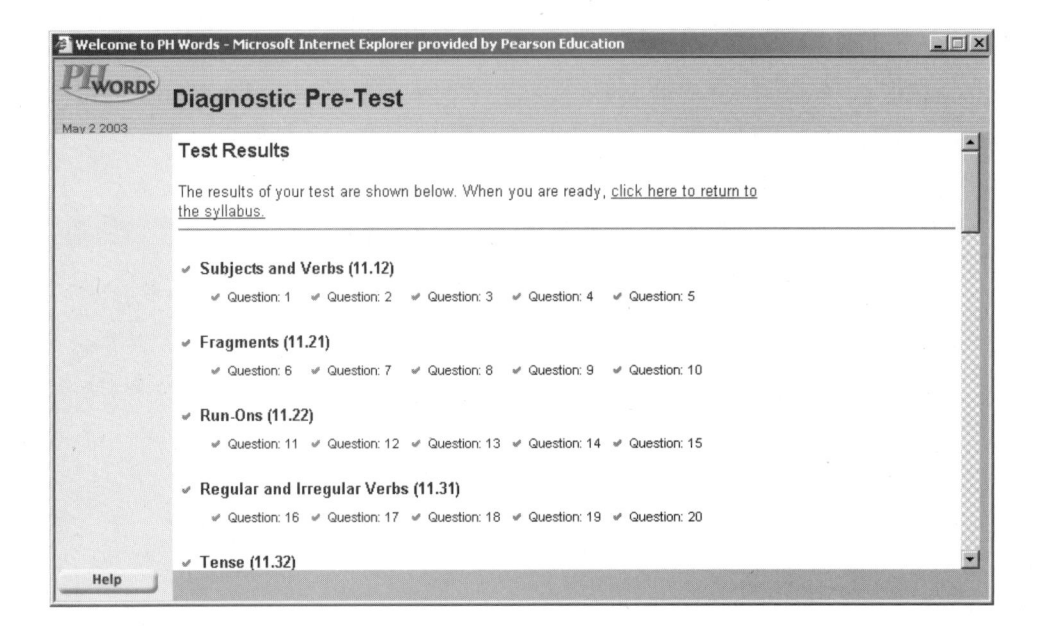

There are several ways these diagnostic results benefit both you and your instructor.

- **Prescriptive Learning Plan**

    If your instructor includes the diagnostic pre-test in the course, your teacher will use the test results to modify your Syllabus by displaying a Mastered icon—
    —next to skills you have mastered. Mastery of a skill requires a minimum of four correct answers out of five. Even if you have achieved mastery, the item will remain in the Syllabus, in case you wish to revisit a mastered grammar lesson at a later time if you or your instructor decide you need a refresher.

- **Progress Reports**

    You can view your overall score on the Diagnostic Pre-Test in the Gradebook, but it is not counted into your grade. However, if you later work on a diagnostically mastered skill that the instructor has chosen to require, your actual score replaces the mastery icon, and it is then counted toward your grade.

- **Diagnostic Reports**

    You also can see your detailed graphical reports with results from the diagnostic test in the Gradebook, along with your own detailed information there.

INSTRUCTOR MESSAGES

When you open the **Course** screen, you will see if you have any messages from your teacher by checking the **Read Messages** link.

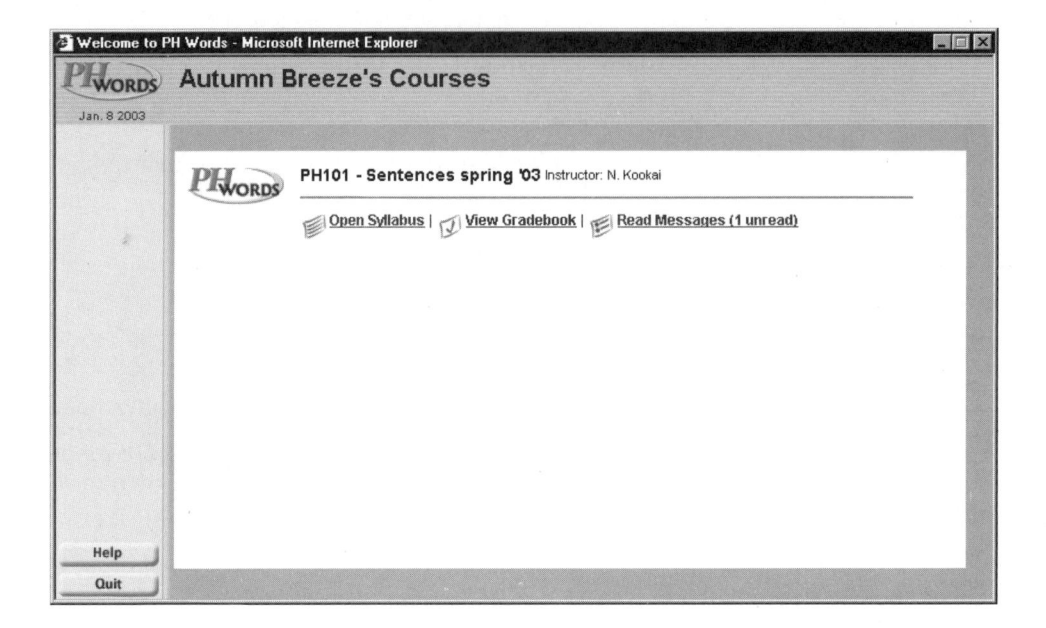

Click the **Read Messages** link to view a list of the messages that have been sent to you.

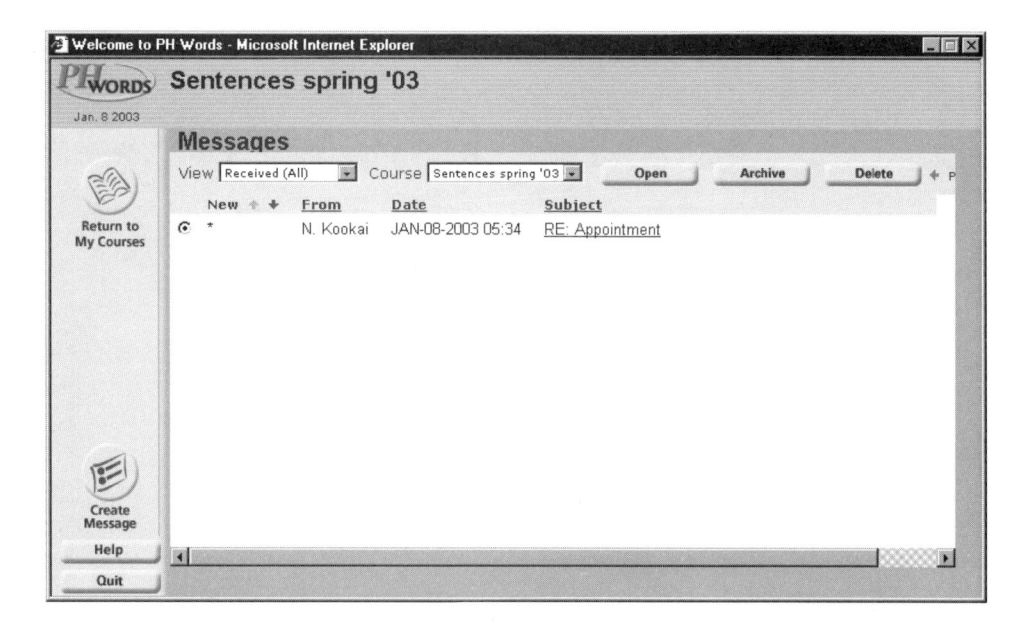

Then click an individual message to read it. Afterwards, you can reopen any message from the **Messages** screen.

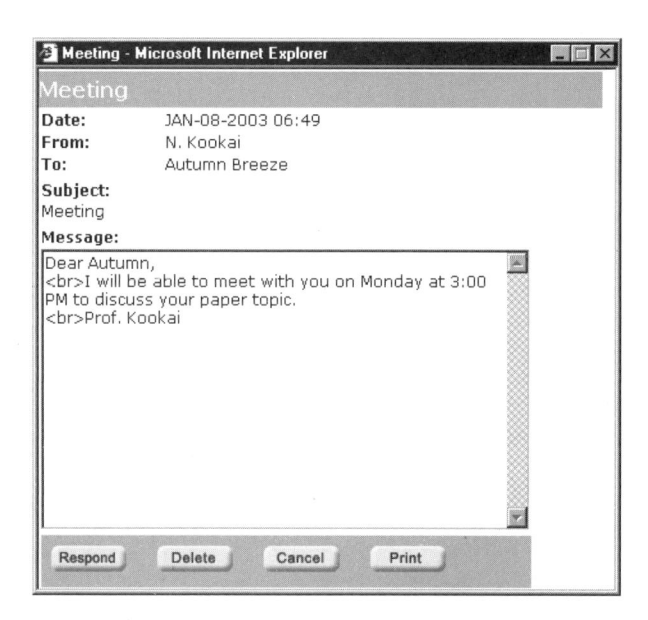

PRINTING THE SYLLABUS

Print your Syllabus by clicking the **Print Syllabus** button on the bottom left side of the **Course** screen.

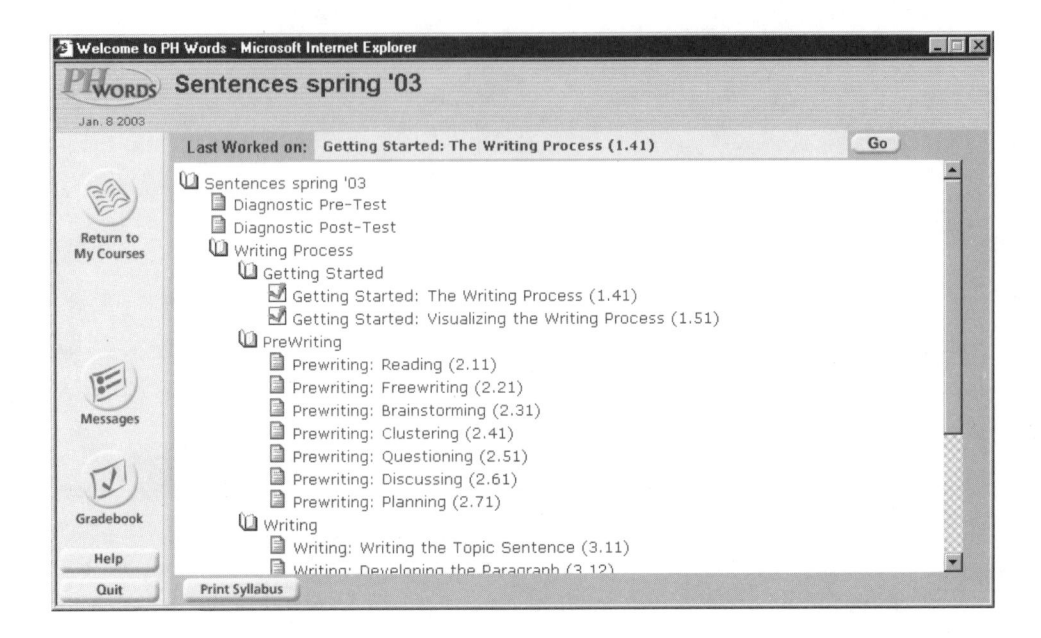

COURSE CONTENT

PH Words covers each basic writing skill in a module — that is, a section —containing four parts:

- Watch video
- Apply exercises
- Recall exercises
- Write exercises

When you open a module for the first time, you will automatically be taken to the **Recall** screen. You can move from one exercise to another by using a set of three tabs at the top of the screen. The tabs open the **Recall**, **Apply,** and **Write** exercises. A separate **Watch** button in the upper right corner opens a pop-up window containing an audio summary and animation of the concept presented in the module. You can return to your Syllabus at any time by clicking the **Return to Syllabus** button. A flag appears on the tab for each exercise that is required.

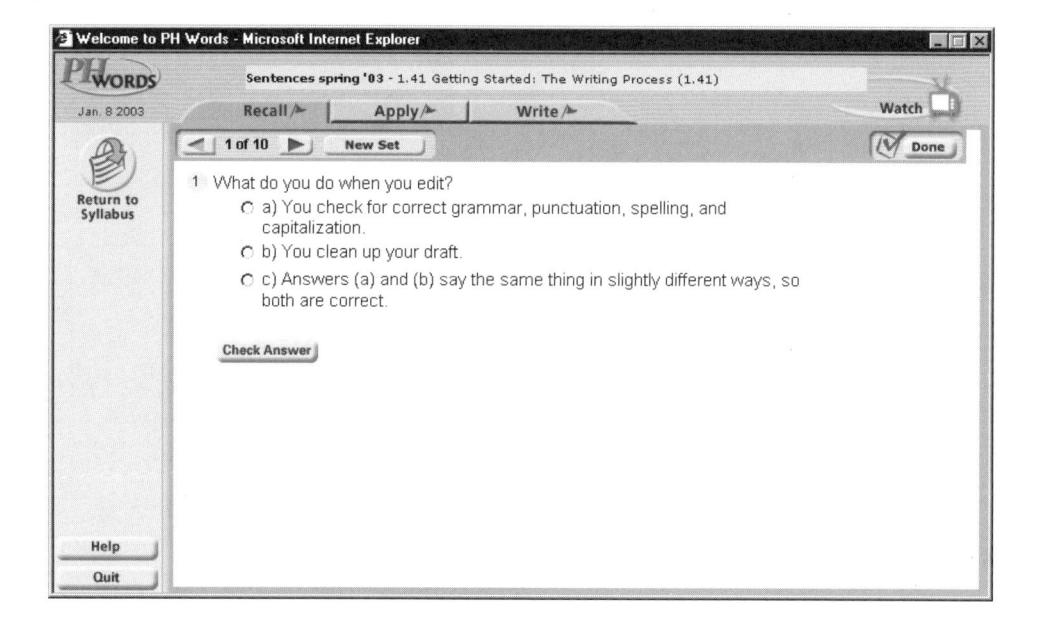

WATCH VIDEO

Watch Videos are short animations intended to refresh your understanding of the skill covered in the module. Watch Videos are intended just for watching; there is no work to be done or response required. They open in a pop-up window, so you can view them at any time as you work through the other parts of each module.

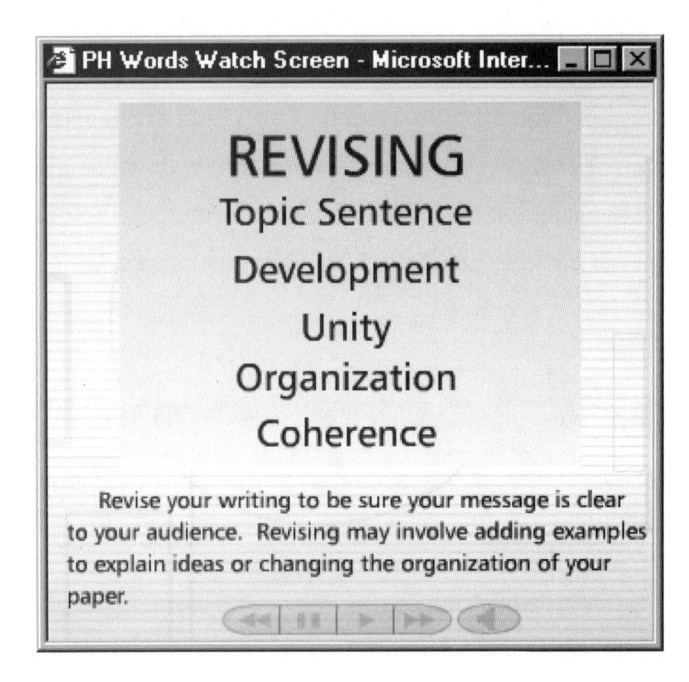

The video and accompanying audio begin playing automatically when the window opens. A custom control bar is grayed out at the bottom of the window so it won't interfere with the animation, but it becomes available for use as soon as you touch it with the cursor.

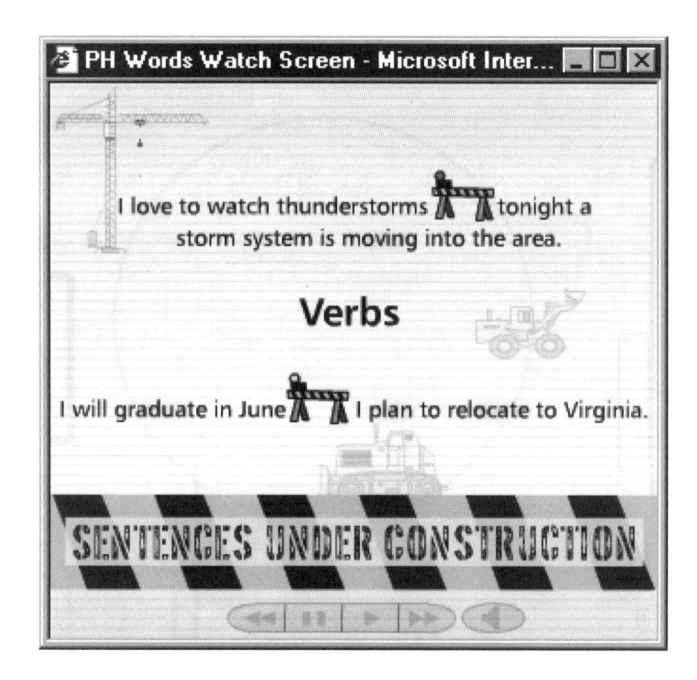

Roll the cursor over the controls to make them active in order to pause, play, rewind, or fast-forward the animation. You can also turn the audio off and on.

RECALL SCREEN

Recall exercises are multiple-choice exercises that check your literal comprehension of the concept in the module. Each Recall screen presents a single question, multiple-choice answers, and a **Check Answer** button. There are ten questions in a set.

You can click any of the answer options on the screen repeatedly, without receiving a score. You can also move from one question to another by clicking the Forward and Back arrows on the left, just below the **Recall Tab**.

These arrows enable you to look at each question in order or skip questions and return to them later. You can select an answer to a question and go back and change it as many times as you like. But when you are comfortable with your answer, you should click **Check Answer**. Once you click **Check Answer**, your answer is locked in, and you cannot try again. The answer then becomes part of your grade.

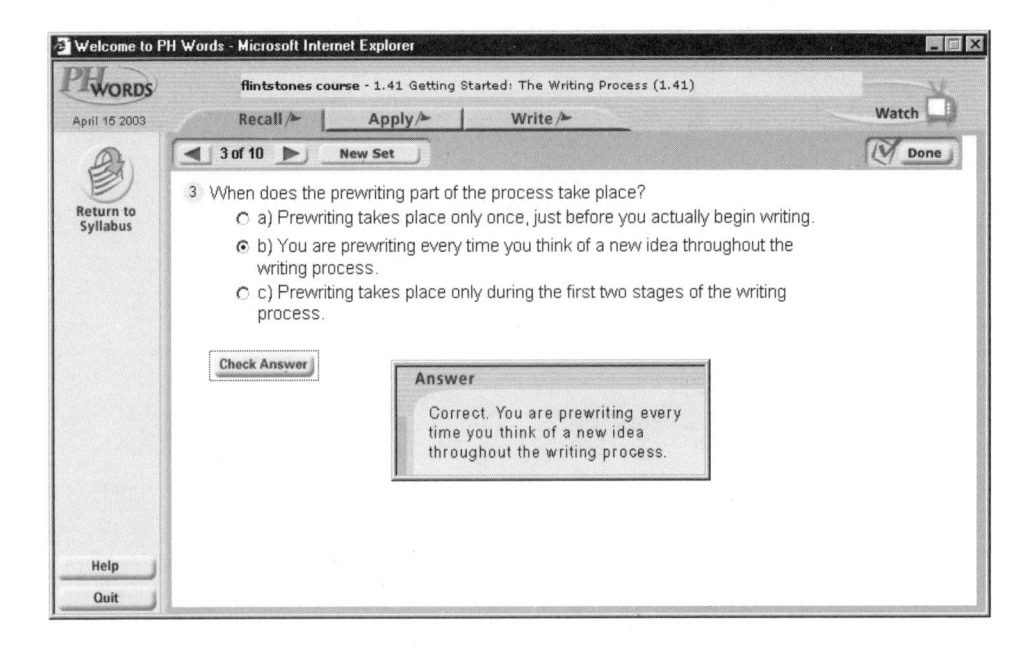

If you answer correctly, PH Words will confirm your answer in a **Correct** box. If you answer incorrectly, PH Words will tell you the answer is **Incorrect**, and then give you the correct answer.

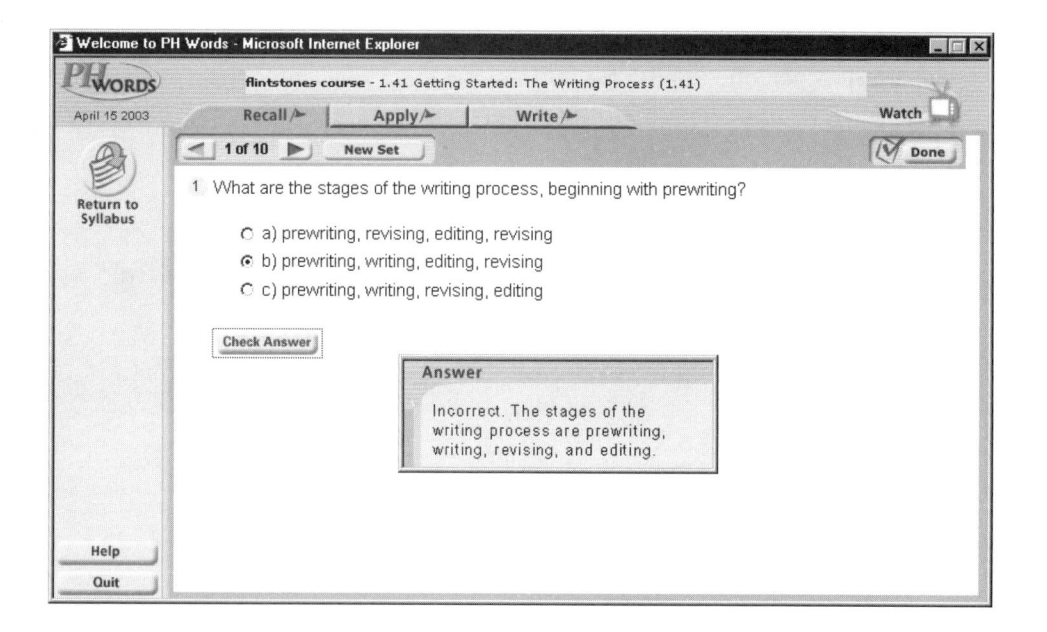

PH Words allows you to work on multiple sets of a Recall exercise and be graded on the last set you complete. However, if your teacher has decided to limit the class to a single set of questions, the **New Set** button will not be available.

When you are finished, click the **Done** button to submit your work. This loads a page showing your score and performance details. From this page, you can print the report, print the entire exercise, or review a specific problem.

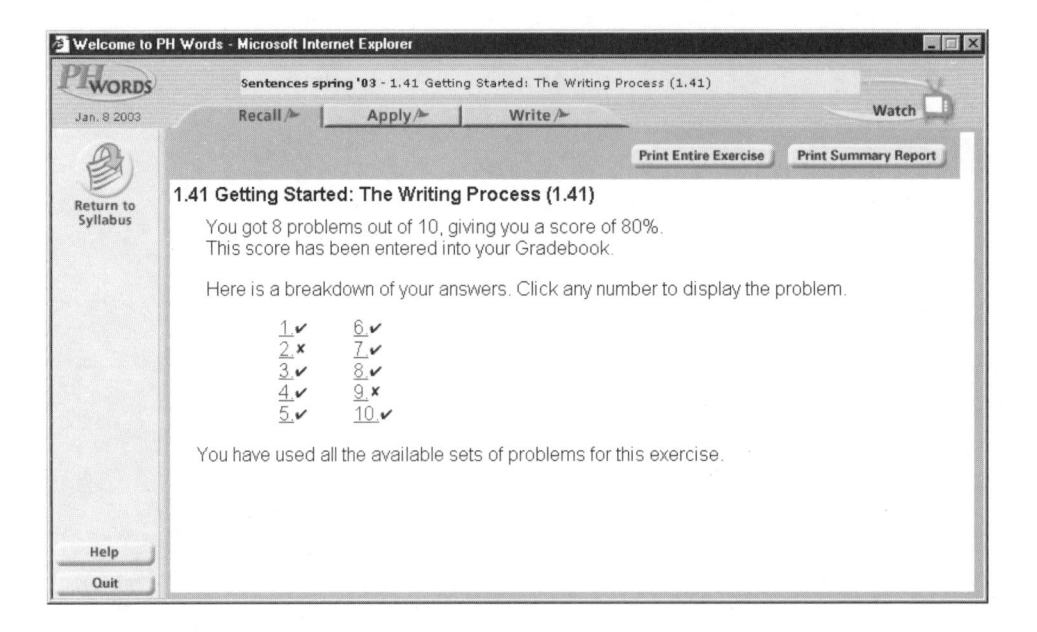

MULTIPLE CHOICE APPLY SCREEN

Each Multiple Choice **Apply** exercise consists of a series of multiple choice questions on the right-hand side of the screen — each referring to a piece of writing shown on the left-hand side of the screen. There is also a **Check Answer** button.

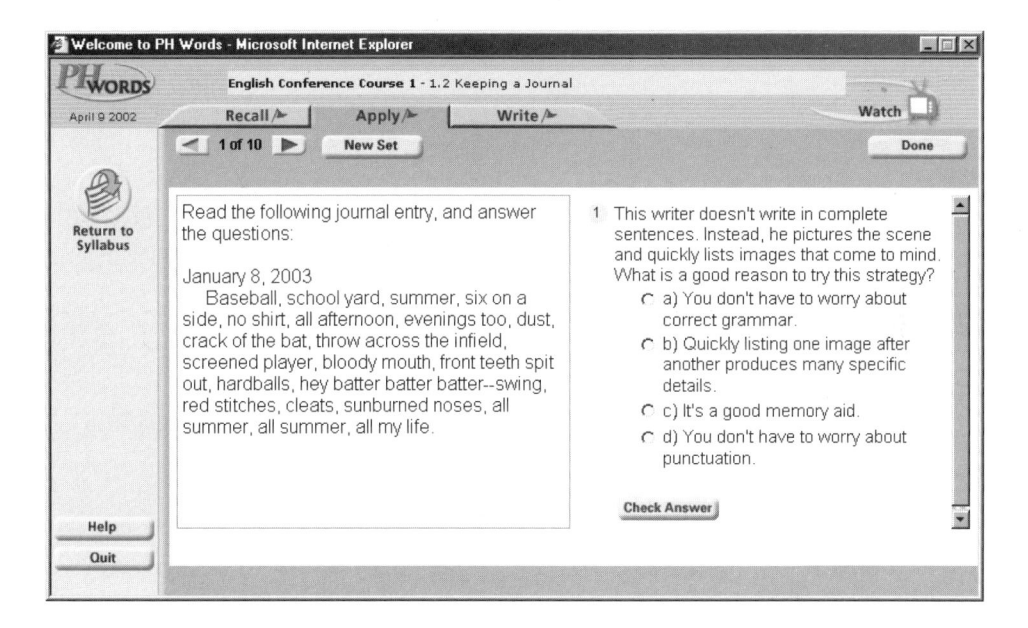

You can click the answer options repeatedly without being scored, but once you click **Check Answer**, you cannot try again. You should click **Check Answer** after you are done with each question.

Move from one question to another by clicking the Forward and Back arrows on the left, just below the **Recall Tab**. These arrows enable you to look at each question in order or skip questions and return to them later. You can select an answer to a question and go back and change it as many times as you like, as long as you have not yet clicked the **Check Answer** button. Once you click **Check Answer**, your answer is locked in and becomes part of your grade.

Once you have clicked **Check Answer**, PH Words will show you a pop-up box indicating if your answer is correct or incorrect. In the multiple choice Apply Section, it will also provide you with the proper "rule" that will help you determine the correct answer.

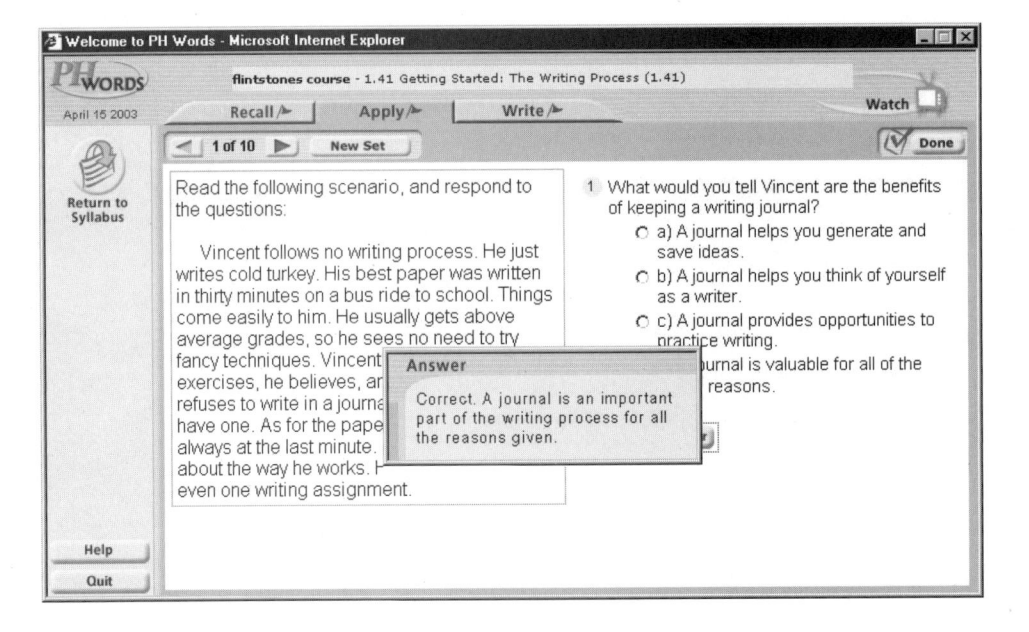

PH Words allows you to work on multiple sets of a Apply exercise and be graded on the last set you complete. However, if your teacher has decided to limit the class to a single set of questions, the **New Set** button will not be available.

Note that as you move from one question to the next in the Apply section, you should pay attention to the piece of writing on the left-hand side of the screen. The writing selection changes every five or ten questions

When you are finished, click the **Done** button to submit your work. This opens a page showing your score and performance details. From this page, you can print the report, print the entire exercise, or review a specific problem.

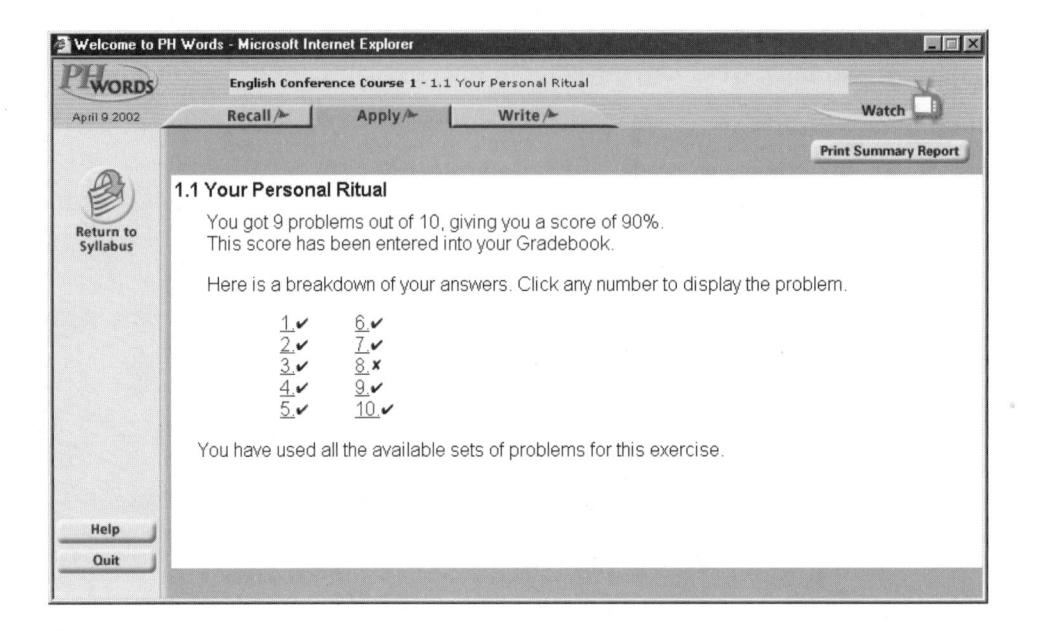

APPLY EXERCISES IN GRAMMAR MODULES

You will find **Apply** exercises featuring tools that allow you to edit writing samples in the area of PH Words that focuses specifically on grammatical issues. In each selection, you must locate and correct up to 10 grammatical errors.

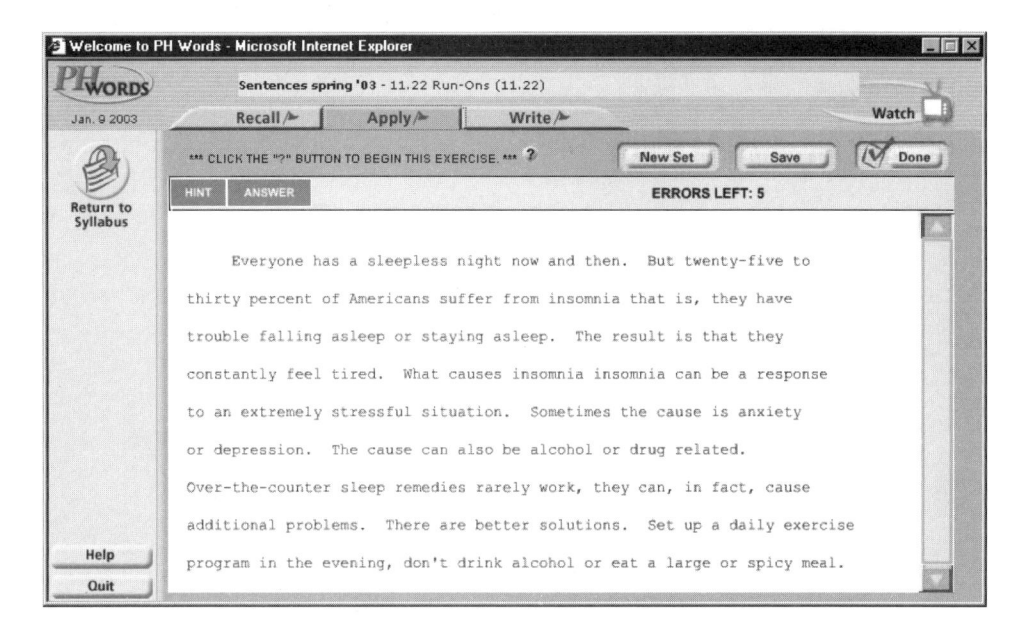

If the selection is longer than 10 lines, you will see a scrollbar on the right. Scroll up and down by clicking the up and down arrows, respectively.

The first thing to do when you open an Apply Grammar exercise is to find the Instruction button located near the top of the screen, just below the three tabs.

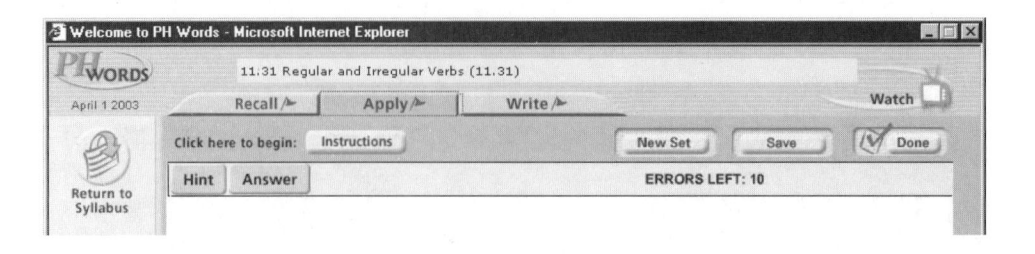

Click the **Instructions** button to see the instructions for the exercise.

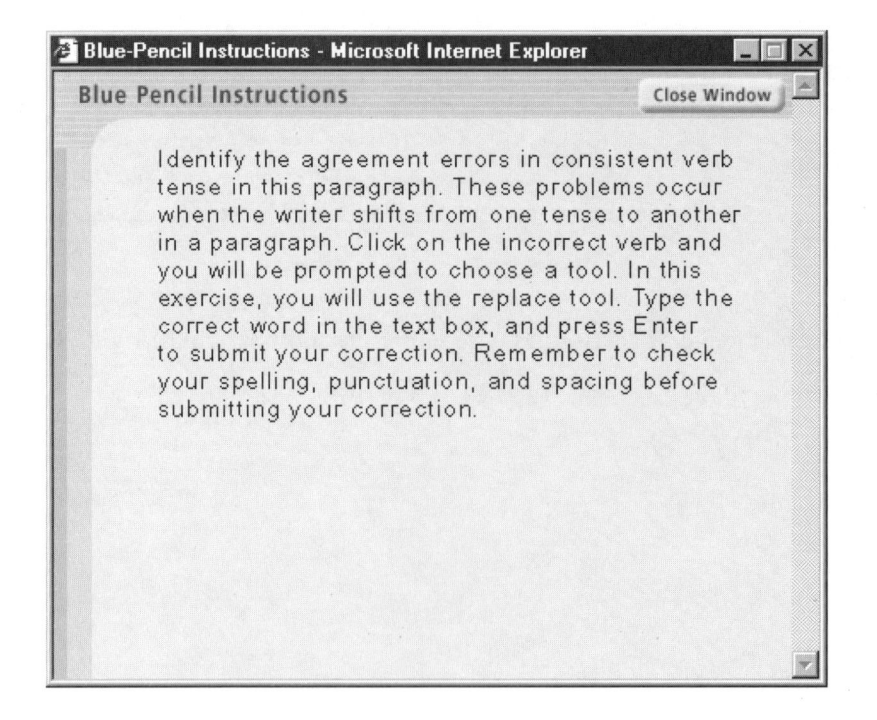

Blue Pencil Instructions

Identify the agreement errors in consistent verb tense in this paragraph. These problems occur when the writer shifts from one tense to another in a paragraph. Click on the incorrect verb and you will be prompted to choose a tool. In this exercise, you will use the replace tool. Type the correct word in the text box, and press Enter to submit your correction. Remember to check your spelling, punctuation, and spacing before submitting your correction.

When you have located an error by clicking it, a **Toolbar** will appear showing icons for one or more Tool options. These icons refer to corrections you might need to make. There are 13 icons available, but not all the icons appear in any one exercise. In fact, in some exercises, there may be just one icon. The icons that appear in a particular exercise are the ones you will need specifically for that exercise.

cs	Comma Splice
id	Identify Tool
frag	Sentence Fragment
fs	Fused Sentence
u	Underline
cap	Capitalize
repl	Replace
del	Delete
ins	Insert
sc	Show Correction
si	Split Infinitive
dm	Dangling Modifier
mm	Misplaced Modifier

You must click the proper correction tool icon, even if there is only one available. Once you select the **Tool**, one of two things will happen:

- You will see a box where you type your answer and press **Enter**, triggering the correct answer to appear in the paragraph.

- You will see the correction in the paragraph text, whether it is an underlined word, a deleted word, or an inserted word.

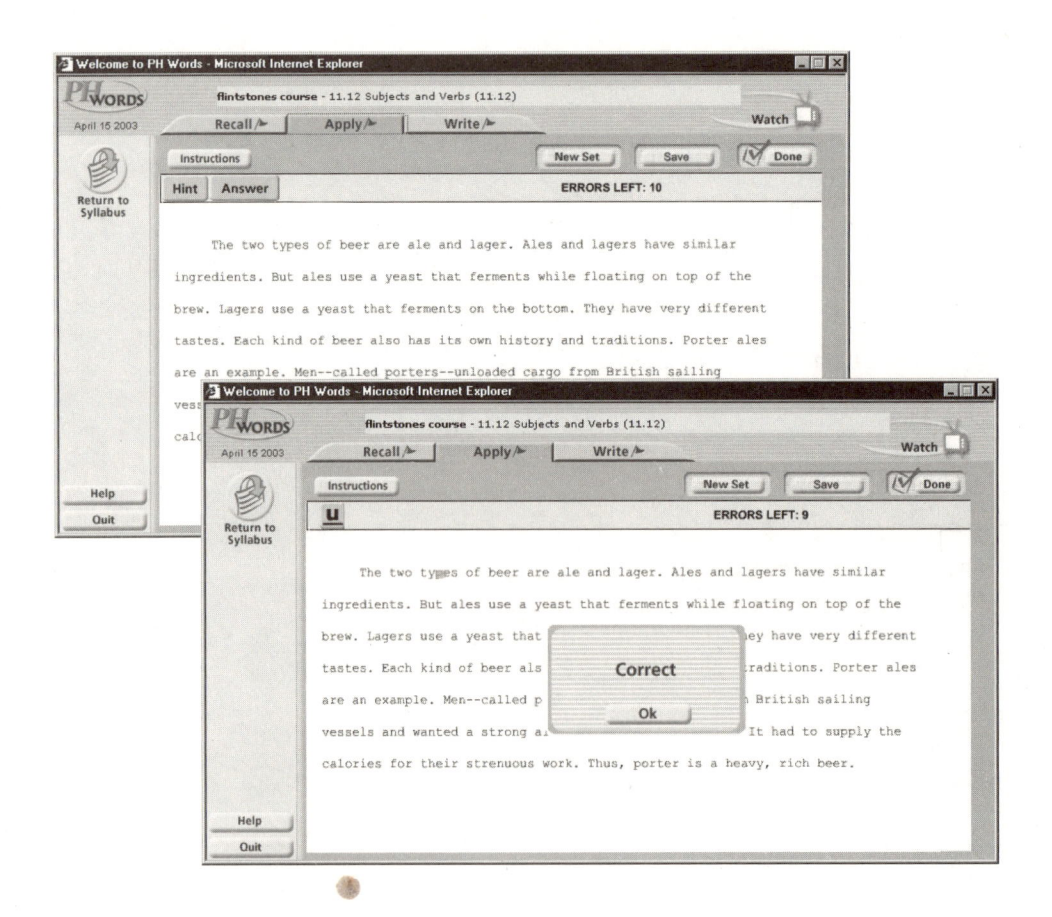

You can request a **Hint** and then an **Answer** for any line of text. Both requests subtract points from your score. You can cancel a **Hint** or **Answer** request before you receive the information by clicking the relevant button again. Canceling the request leaves the score as is.

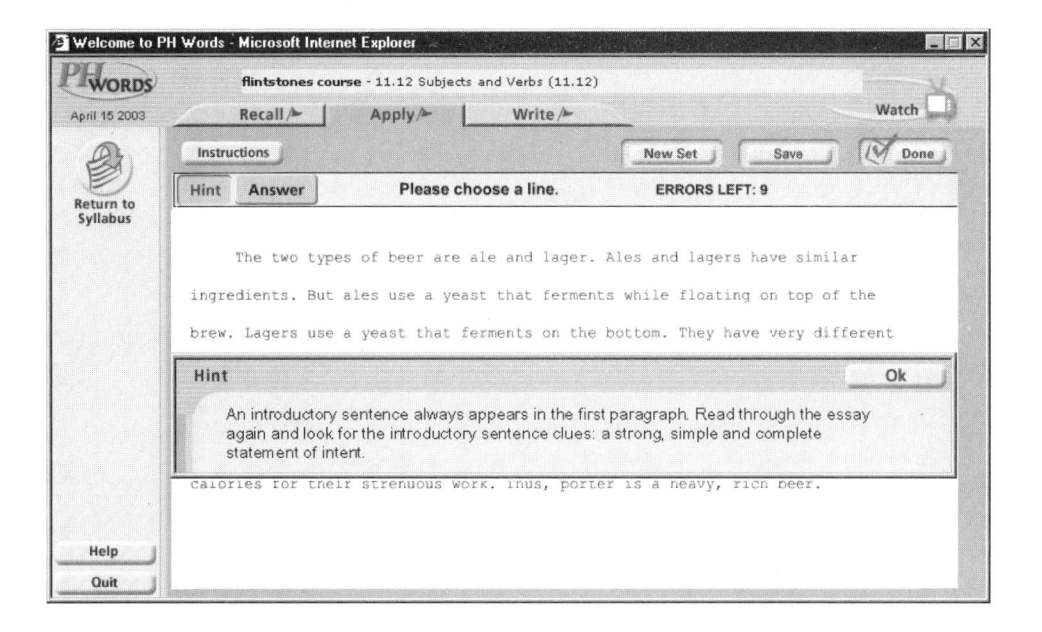

Clicking the **Hint** button opens a dialogue box giving an appropriate suggestion about the answer. Clicking the **Answer** button places the correct answer above the incorrect form.

Remember, you must select **Hint** before you can request **Answer**.

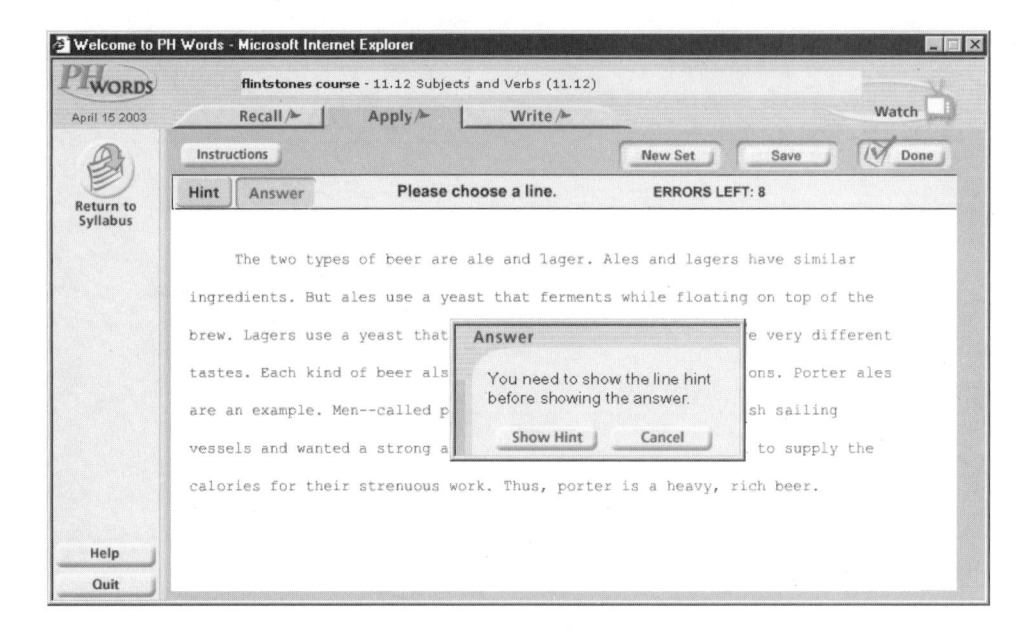

By clicking **New Set**, you can attempt multiple sets of these Apply exercises, but you will be graded on the last set you complete. However, if your teacher has decided to limit the class to a single set of questions, the **New Set** button will be hidden.

When you are finished, click the **OK** button to submit your work. This loads a page showing your score and performance details. From this page, you can print the report, print the entire exercise, or review a specific problem.

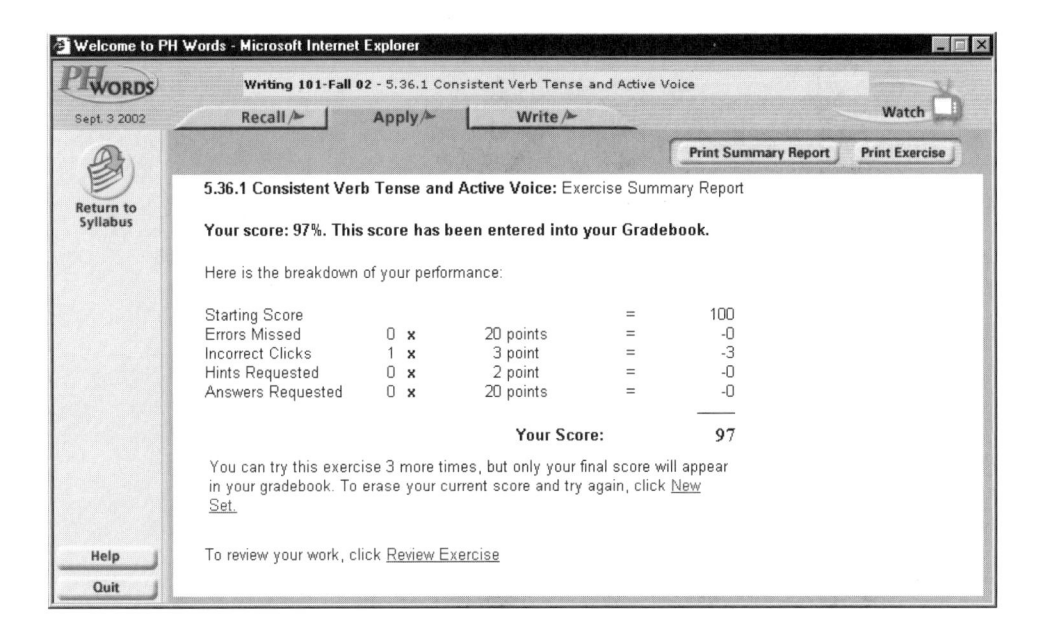

WRITE EXERCISES

Write exercises ask you to demonstrate your understanding of the grammar topic by writing a paragraph or an essay. You submit these exercises to your instructor, who will then provide feedback and assign grades.

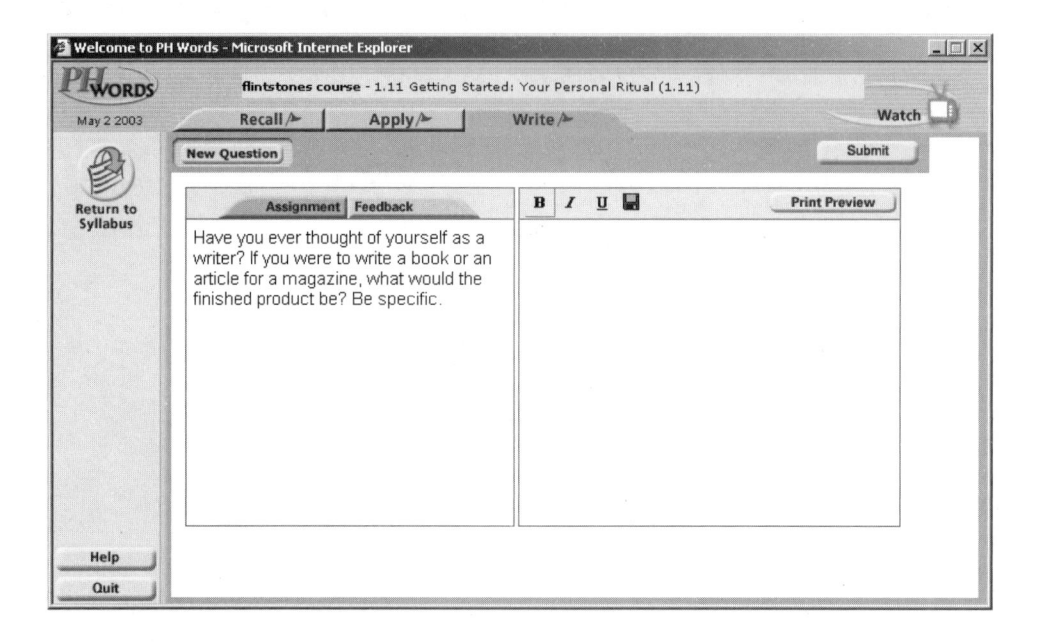

There are two views associated with **Write** screens:

- Assignment
- Feedback

ASSIGNMENT VIEW

When you first open a **Write** exercise, the screen appears in **Assignment** view, with the Assignment tab chosen and an assignment showing on the left side of the screen. These assignments may be text only or they may include diagrams.

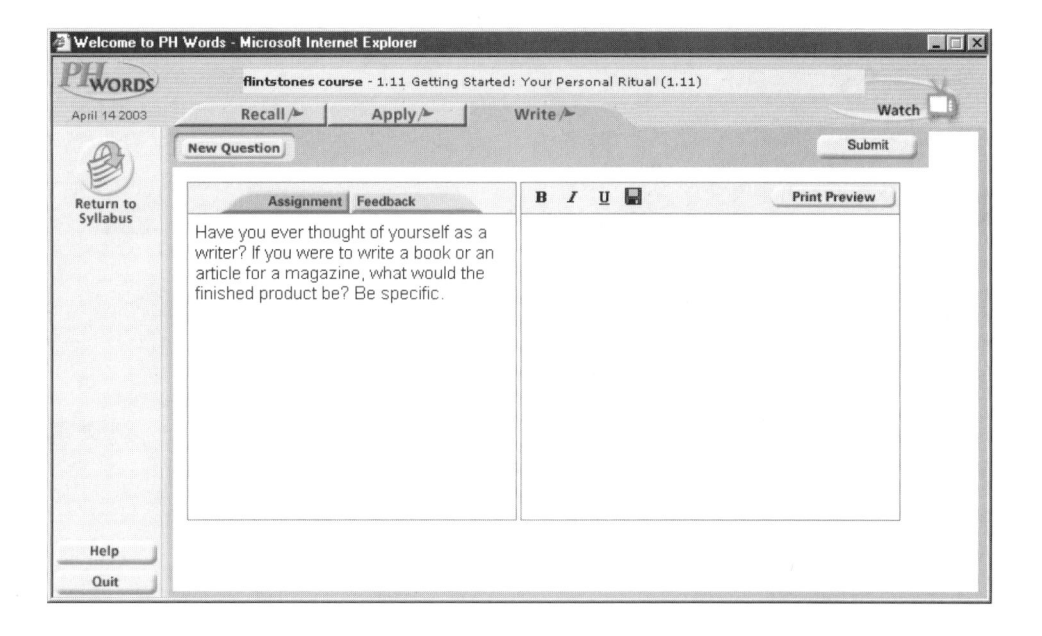

With diagrams, there will always be an **Enlarge** button. Clicking **Enlarge** will pop open a full-size view of the diagram in a new window. You can move the window below or beside the assignment window so you can still see it while you write.

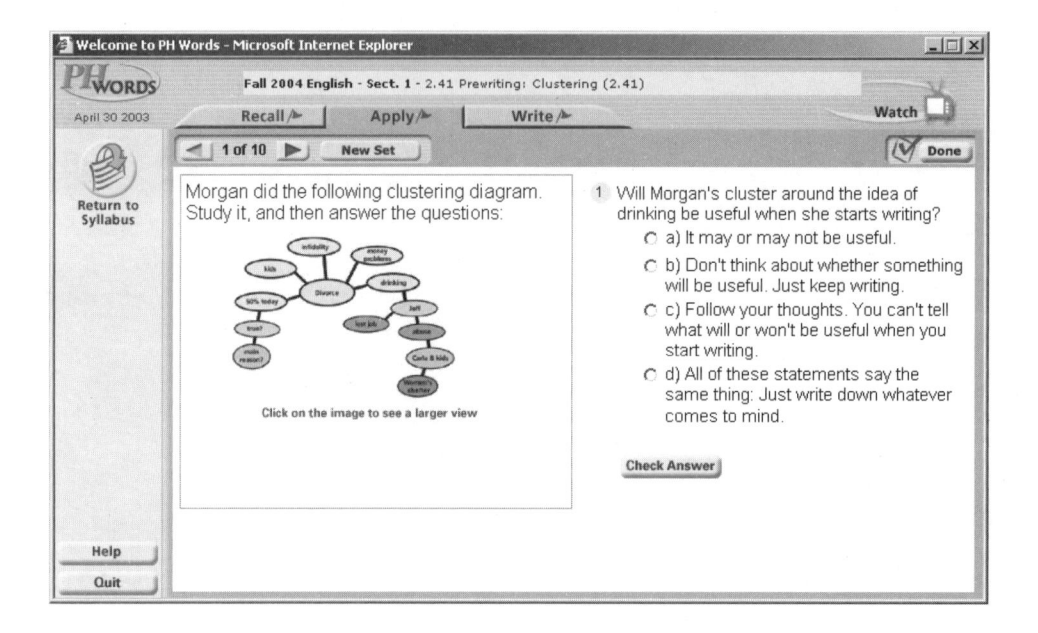

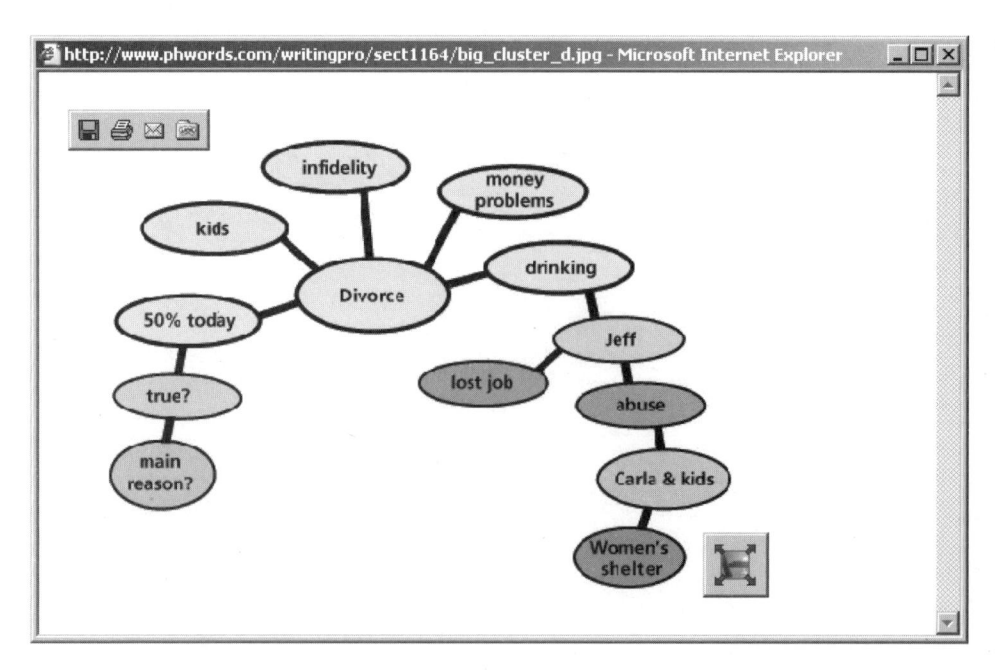

By default, you can view all of the questions available in a specific Write exercise, one-by-one, and then choose one to complete. Click the **New Question** button to cycle through the questions before beginning to write. However, if your teacher has decided to limit you a single question, the **New Question** button will be hidden.

At any time, you can click a **Print Preview** button to see your work in a new window. From here you can close or print the assignment. When you are finished, click the **Done** button to submit your work.

FEEDBACK VIEW

Once you have submitted your work, the screen switches to **Feedback** view, with the Feedback tab "on" and the Done, and New Question buttons hidden.

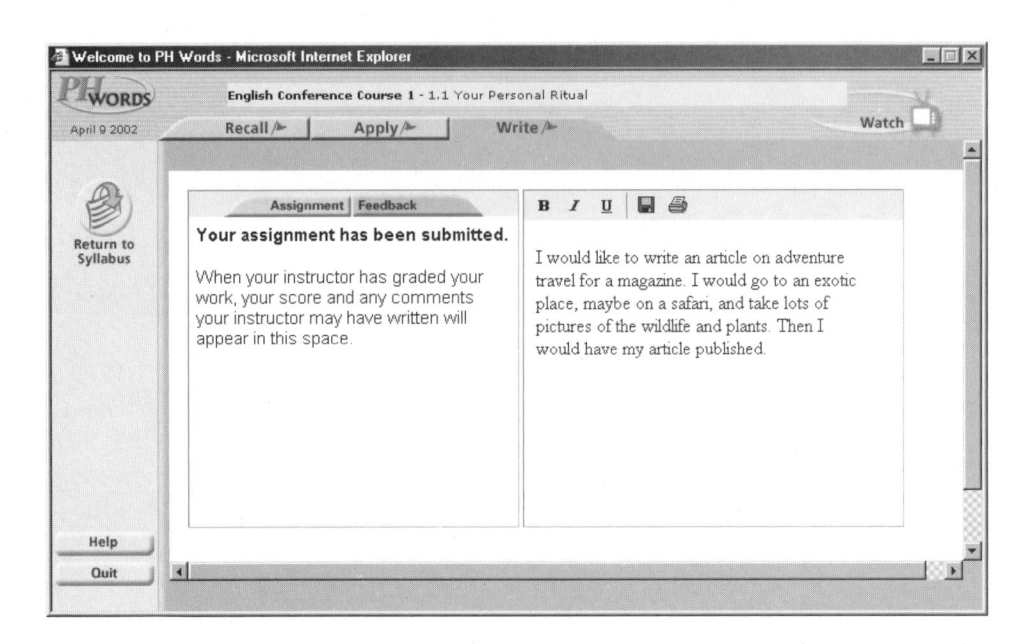

After submitting an assignment, you will see an automatic message in the feedback area indicating that your assignment has been submitted and that your instructor will send feedback later. At the same time, the module's Syllabus icon changes to the Submitted icon — — indicating that you have submitted the exercise to your teacher and are awaiting a response.

When your teacher has graded and returned your work, the module's Syllabus icon changes to the Graded icon — .. You can now view the instructor's comments and your grade by reopening the exercise.

GRADEBOOK SCREEN

You can view your own scores and performance data in the **Gradebook**. Open yours by clicking the **Gradebook** button in the sidebar of the Syllabus screen. The button displays a checkmark when there is new grade data for you to review, and reverts to an empty icon when you have seen all data in the Gradebook.

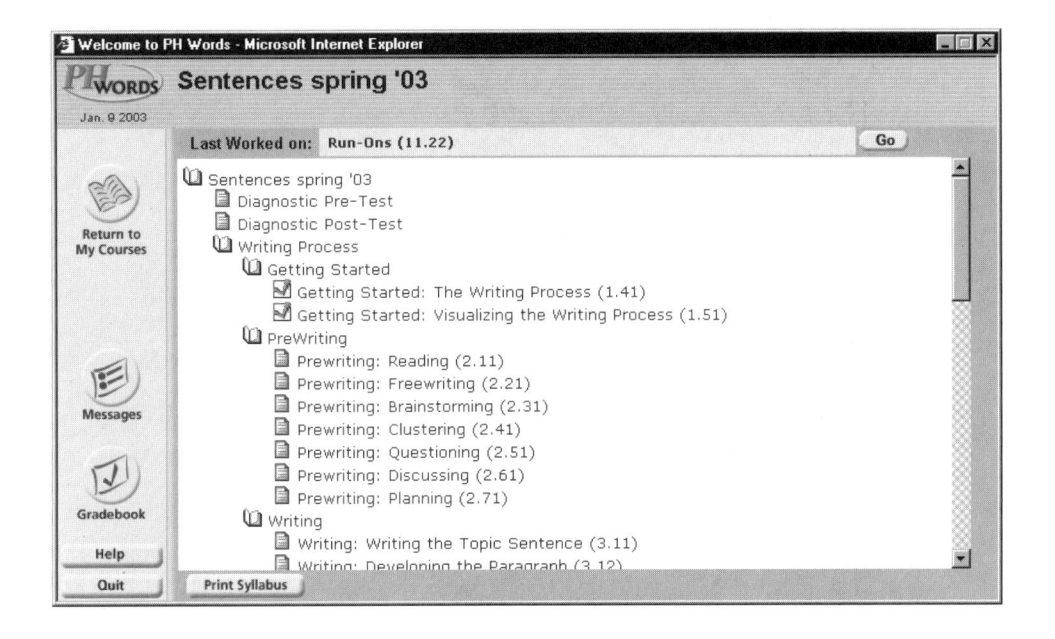

You can also open the **Gradebook** from the **Courses** screen. Here, the **Gradebook** link will also display a checkmark if there is new data for you to review.

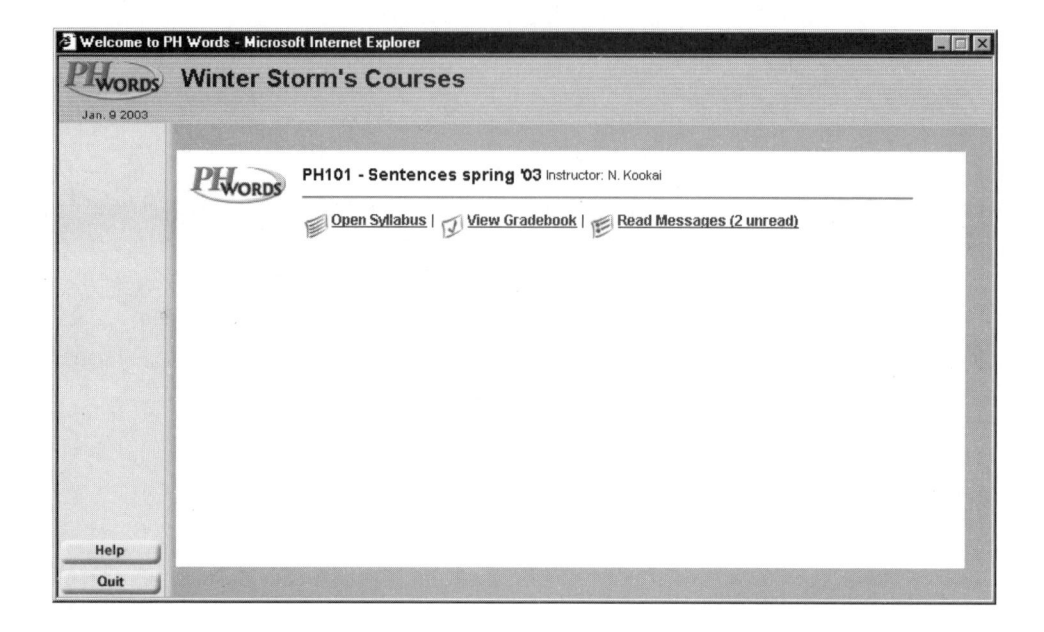

The Gradebook report will include the information your instructor has selected for each content item, including some or all of these areas:

- Total score for the item
- Number of questions correct
- Number of questions incorrect
- Time-on-task
- Date the item was last opened
- Number of sets completed

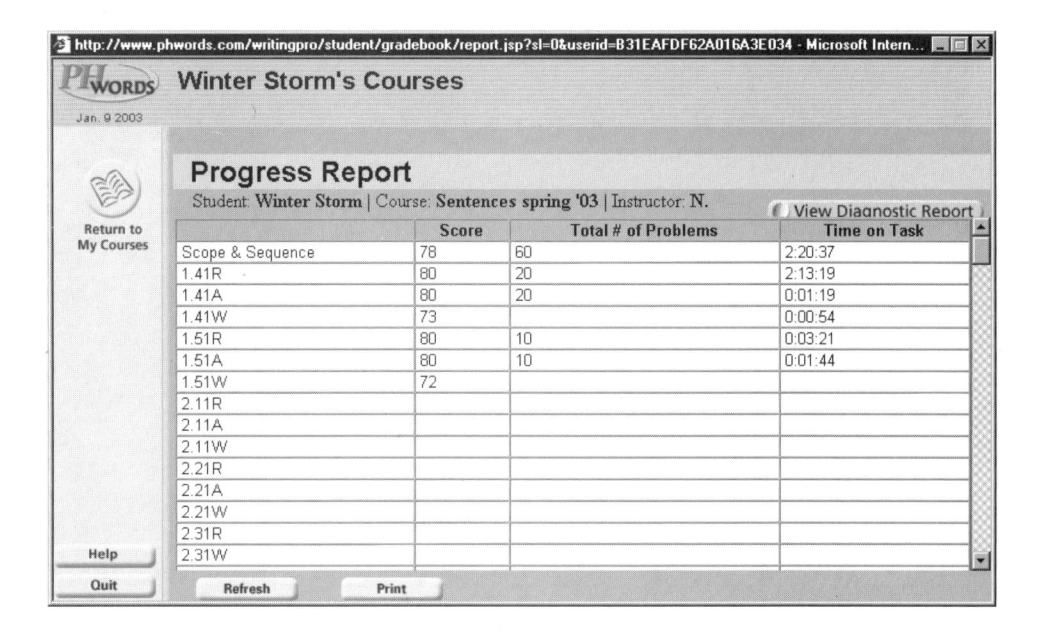

Content items that are not required appear in the report in blue. Items that you mastered on the diagnostic pretest appear in green and show a score of one hundred percent. A key at the bottom explains this color-coding.

Gradebook data are updated automatically once a day—overnight—but you can click the **Refresh** button at the bottom of the report to see any results submitted since the last update.

MESSAGES SCREEN

You can send messages to your teacher through the PH Words messaging system. Click the **Messages** button in the sidebar on the Syllabus screen to access the Messaging system.

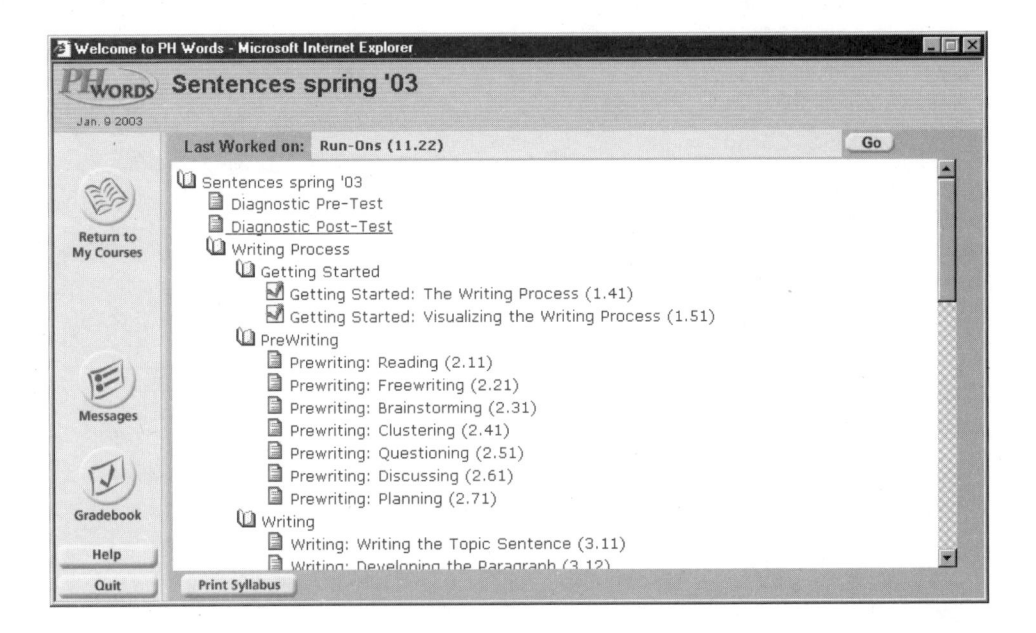

CREATING MESSAGES

You can create messages by clicking the **Create Message** button on the left side of the **Messages** screen. The button opens a **Compose Message** window that contains all the information you need to create and send a message.

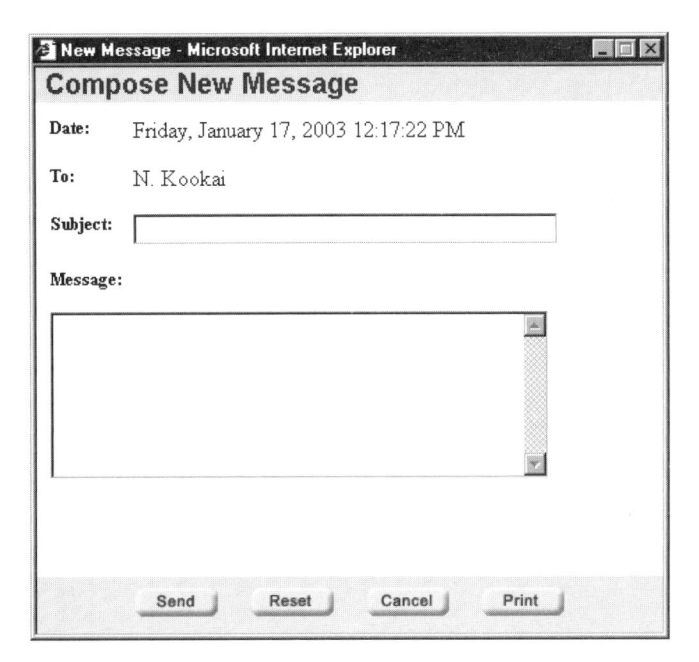

READING MESSAGES

You can read messages either by clicking the subject of a message on the main Messages screen or by selecting the message and clicking the **Open** button. Both of these methods open the message in a new window.

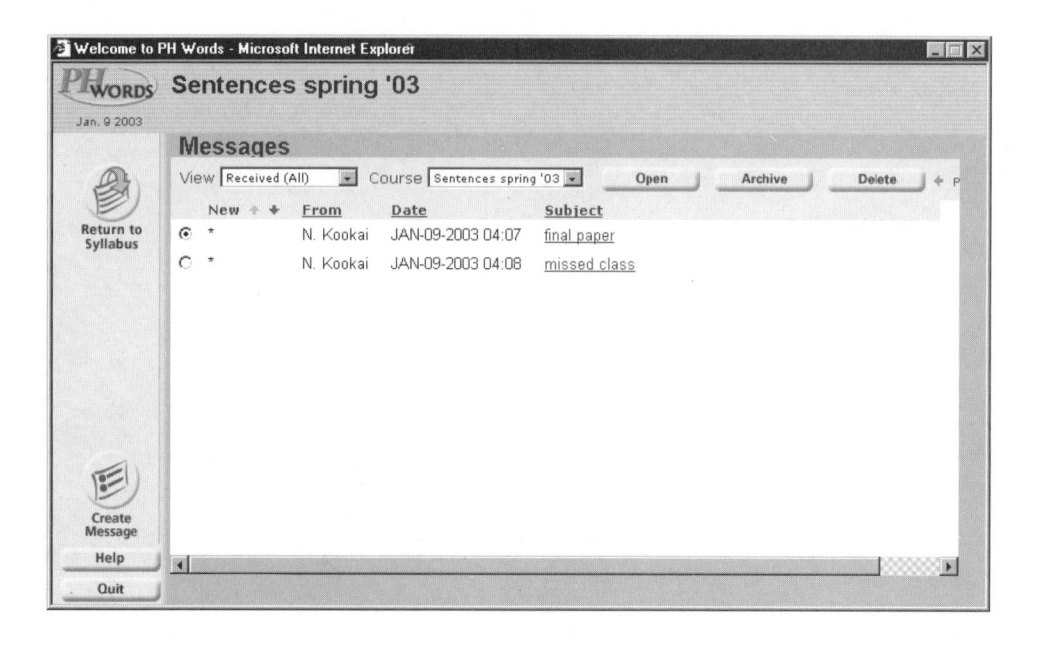

You can choose among your messages using the **View** drop-down list. The Views include several choices:

- Received (All)
- Sent
- Received (Unread)
- Archived

In addition, if you are enrolled in more than one course, you can organize your messages by using the Course drop-down list. You can sort messages in a variety of ways by clicking the column headings on the Messages screen. Each sort category displays up and down arrows when selected to enable sorting in reverse order.

MANAGING MESSAGES

You can archive messages to save them in a separate folder. Select the message and click the **Archive** button. Then you can access Archived messages by selecting the Archived option in the View drop-down list. You can print a copy of any message by clicking the Print button when the message is open. Delete messages that you don't want to save by selecting the message and clicking the **Delete** button.

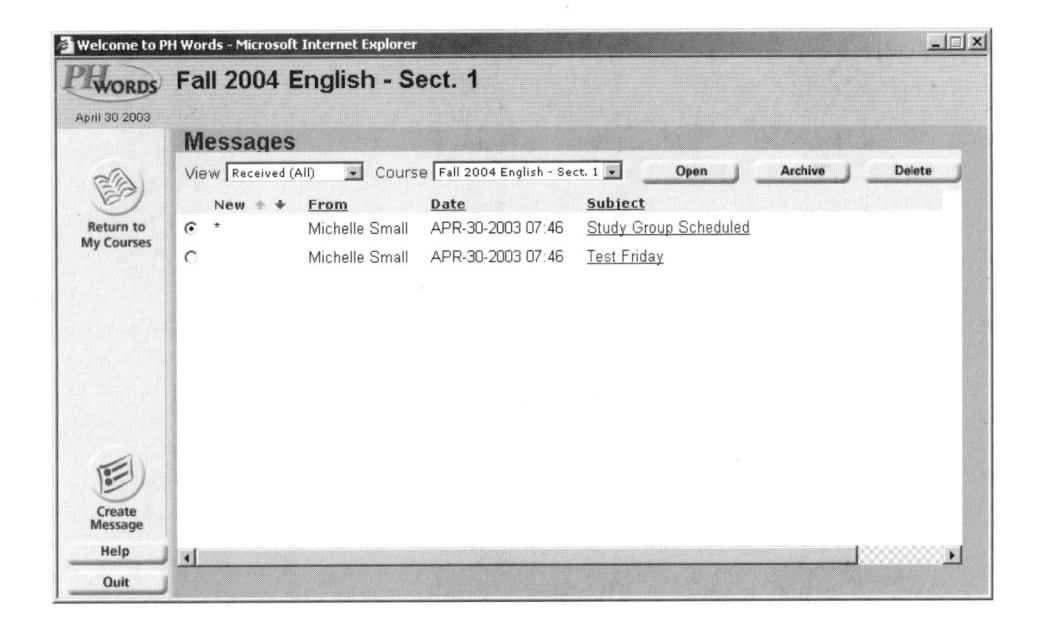

PRODUCT HELP

Orientations include animated screens that introduce the course and explain how to use the program. Each tour consists of at least one animated screen. When multiple screens are included, the screens change automatically. The tours may include audio and video.

Orientations always appear under their own heading at the beginning of a syllabus. When you use the product for the first time, the Syllabus appears with this heading expanded and all others collapsed.

Online Help is available anywhere in the product. Note that this information comes from Prentice Hall and not your school or the instructor.

Clicking any **Help** button will bring you information about the topic showing on the screen where you clicked. There is a lot of information on some of the Help pages and you may need to scroll down to find the specific topic you are looking for. This online help covers both the use of PH Words and your navigation through the program.

FOR TECHNICAL SUPPORT, PLEASE CALL THE
PRENTICE HALL MEDIA SUPPORT LINE
1-800-677-6337
MONDAY THROUGH FRIDAY
8:00 AM TO 5:00 PM CST
OR E-MAIL US AT
media.support@pearsoned.com

FOR THE MOST RECENT
INFORMATION AND UPDATES ON PH WORDS, VISIT
www.phwords.com/support

PH Words Development Team

Designers	Dave Roh and Laura Juitt
Executive Producer	Philip Lanza
Product Manager	Michelle Small
Production	Peter Silvia and John Coco
Art and Media	Greg Lamb, Joshua Sutherland, Chris Lynch

Editorial Team

Editor in Chief	Leah Jewell
Associate Editor In Chief, Development	Rochelle Diogenes
Senior Acquisitions Editor	Craig Campanella
Senior Marketing Manager	Rachel Falk
Senior Media Editor	Christy Schaack
Development Editor	Harriett Prentiss
Copy Editor	Nancy Kukura

Content Development Team

Content Developer/Writer . . . . Veronica Tomaiuolo

Content Providers:
- Peter England, Blinn College
- Evelyn Kelly, Coastal Carolina Community College
- Lisa Windham, McLennan Community College
- Kim Zernechel, Minneapolis Technical and Community College
- Lina Brotherton, Oakton Community College
- Susan Cunningham, Ohlone College
- Tim Jones, Oklahoma State University
- Steve Jaech, Pierce College
- Ann Ritchey, Pierce College
- DeVry-Dupage, Tidewater Community College
- Christine Lewinski, Tidewater Community College
- Betty Perkinson, Tidewater Community College
- Tina Margolis, Westchester Community College
- Rebecca Hewett
- Bruce Thaler